Value-driven
Risk and agility

J. ALPHEY

ISBN: 1533342008
ISBN-13: 978-1533342003

Contents

Preface

We read about failing projects every day. Sometimes these projects seem to have started with no robust plan, missing activities or underestimating the complexity of the problem to be solved. Maybe they began implementation too early, before the problem was understood. You can look at these projects, at least in retrospect, as "failures in planning".

However for many failed projects this doesn't seem to be the cause of failure. The project team have invested time in planning at the start, but then something changes. Perhaps an unexpected factor is found, or the project isn't delivering the expected benefits, or new and changing requirements are added. The plan becomes out of date and needs to be changed. But somehow the level of change overwhelms the team. They struggle to both deliver the project and manage the change.

These can be considered "Red Queen's Race" failures.

> *here, you see, it takes all the running you can do,*
> *to keep in the same place*
>
> **The Red Queen,**
> **"Through the Looking-Glass", Lewis Carroll**

The motivation for this book came from my experiences in running project training between 2013 and 2016. The delegates asked me to focus on the key, practical areas which added the most value and so the "Value-driven" approach was born. As I worked more with these teams, the questions shifted from "how do we build a plan?" to "how do we apply the plan in the real world?". And those "real world" questions typically came down to change. If you don't know all of the answers and you expect a level of change, is it still possible to succeed? How can you plan for what might go wrong? How can you plan to seize your opportunities?

This book is intended for anyone who would like to move on from just building a plan. Those who need to plan in a changing environment, whether they see themselves as planners, they give inputs into plans, or they need to use the plans of others. These techniques apply at many levels in a project, from a program(me) manager building a set of stages which will be implemented as projects, to a team leader structuring the work of a small team.

About this book

Over the years 1999 to 2016 I held a range of Project Director roles at a UK-based semiconductor company. I shall call it "ChipCo" to keep it anonymous. Over this time, this grew from a small organisation almost entirely in the UK to a thriving and highly profitable FTSE100 multinational with 30 sites. I led the project management team in the core semiconductor design business and then owned and developed the corporate approach to project management.

This book is a sequel to "Value-Driven Project Planning" (ISBN 1-5330-5992-6). My previous book shared some of the learning and experiences of teams that I have worked with. It covered effective project planning approaches and outlined four key sets of project management tools for dealing with different environments. I refer to these as "**The four horsemen of project planning**"

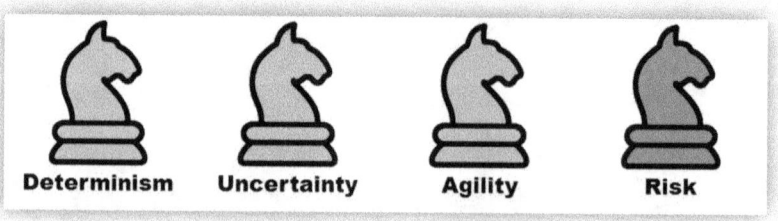

Figure 1 – The "Four Horsemen of Project Planning"

The previous book covered the first two of these. It focuses on a stable planning environment and introduces the key tools of planning.

Determinism – Planning where the work is known, or at least knowable.

Uncertainty – Planning when we agree what we want to do but it is harder to predict what will happen as a result.

This book looks at the last two areas. These arise as the project environment becomes more complex with more interactions and less ability to see cause and effect.

Risk – Planning to reduce the impact of unexpected change on the project.

Agility – Planning to exploit change to maximize value.

Risk and agility may seem like odd partners. Risk Management is seen as part of the classical project management tradition of large projects. "Agile" is often seen as a movement rebelling against those classical approaches. But both are about change. The complex project environment becomes fast changing as priorities shift, market needs change and customers clamour for attention. The illusion of control from detailed planning, characterized by project managers with Gantt Charts, may be lost.

> *Outcomes emerge in the interplay of everyone's plans and intentions and no one can control the interplay.*
>
> *Ralph D. Stacey,*
> ***Complexity and Organizational Reality***

> *One lesson that we learned was that a plan is, at best, a model. A skilled team could put together a great plan that would give them a high chance of success, but they could not truly predict the future. The hard part was asking the question "What if?". Not "what do we want to happen?" but "what might happen?"*

This way of thinking changes the whole nature of planning. You cannot focus only on one plan, but the team need to keep thinking about what might happen, and what they will do about that, and what might happen then.

This doesn't mean that planning has no value. It means that a single plan is not enough. The work that goes into planning does not stop with one plan but continues through the project with multiple plans, plan revisions and alternate management plans. The phrase I used to keep on my wall is below:

> *Plans are nothing, planning is everything*
>
> *Dwight D. Eisenhower*

I make no claim to having invented the techniques that I am describing in this book. Risk Management is a well-established discipline and accepted in many forms as a key part of managing projects. Agile planning is also a well-adopted set of approaches. What the book is doing is to extend the approach for planning introduced in the previous book. This looks at how we can deal better with change, both protecting from disaster and exploiting opportunities.

Acknowledgements

This book is inspired by my own experiences and would never have existed without the talented teams that I have worked with and the constant learnings that I took away from project interactions. I learned something new about projects and teams constantly. I learned even more when I had the chance to sit in another office halfway across the world and work with a team on what we could share and learn from their latest project. My thanks to all of the teams who welcomed me and shared their thinking. It seems almost unfair to single out individuals or groups, but special thanks to a few people at "ChipCo", with no diminishing of my gratitude to others.

To the Austin team for evenings idea-swapping at the Salt Lick and to the Bangalore team for showing me the power and energy of self-belief, to Tudor for reminding me what is on the card, Ken for being honest, John for often seeing it like I do, Shyam for showing me that there is always good beer if you know where to look and to Steve for getting me writing.. And thanks to Paul, Steve, John and Susan for reviewing the book.

More than anyone, my thanks to Liz, Tristan and Jack for making the journey worthwhile.

We are uncovering better ways of developing ...
by doing it and helping others do it

The Agile Manifesto

Examples and principles

Project management is all about practical application. As well as good practice, this book will include some of my own experiences with project planning. We didn't get everything right, but we tried to learn from the mistakes even more than the successes.

 Project experiences are shown in the text like this. These are the "narrative" of the book and discuss what I have personally experienced with the teams with which I've worked. Both the good and the less good.

I have always found that others have put key ideas more elegantly than I could hope to do. In the tradition of "standing on the shoulders of giants" I hope you will find the included quotes relevant and thought-provoking.

> *Quotes are shown in the text like this.*

Key principles, advice and tools suggestions are highlighted in the text when they occur.

Key principles are shown in the text like this.

This book is intended be interesting and enjoyable. It is not meant to be a text book full of problems to wade through. However, this symbol marks suggested places to take some time and think about examples from your own projects and how the ideas might apply.

Chapter 1

What is "Value-driven"?

In the book "Value-driven Project Planning" I outlined the concept of "Value-driven" in project management. High value activities focus on the project and the people more than on adherence to standardised rules. Administrative activities, often focused on generic rules, typically offer lower value to the business.

There are many project methodologies in use. Each has their own set of rules and language. These include the Bodies of Knowledge (BoKs) from APM (Association for Project Management) and PMI (Project Management Institute), Prince2, AgilePM and Scrum Alliance to name but a few. And using standardised language, stages, documents and rules brings consistency to an organisation

Value-driven Project Management is about focusing on the areas which give the most value to you and to your business. Above all, Value-driven Project Management is pragmatic. It's easy to get distracted into rules, process and measuring compliance and to forget that these aren't the end goal, which is to deliver value to the business, using projects as a method to achieve this.

> Project Management skills are valuable and applicable to everyone working on projects.

Chapter 2

Finding a cloud in the silver lining

Managing Risk is natural

Risk Management is not an esoteric project management practice. Like planning, it is as natural as breathing and we all engage in it every day. Look at the example below, which represents Risk Management in normal life.

 *You have some visitors around for coffee but you are out of stock of your favourite biscuits. One of your children has volunteered to go to the local store to buy some more. But there is a busy road in between. He or she could cross the road or they could choose to use the footbridge. They evaluate two alternate plans (cross directly or use the footbridge). The "cross directly" option gets them to the shops faster. However they consider the risk of injury. To do this they use historic data to assess the likely level of traffic and so the likelihood of injury, considering the severity of the outcome were you to be hit by a car. They also consider the urgency of the errand and the impact of delay by using the footbridge. Having assessed the tradeoff involved they determine that on this occasion the best solution is to take the lower risk option and use the footbridge.*

The shopper may not write this down formally. Indeed he or she may not be consciously making Risk-driven choices but we are making these decisions throughout our lives. Indeed it is fair to say that *every* decision is a tradeoff of Risk and reward. With project Risk Management we are making the process more formal and more visible. This allows us more consciously to assess the consequences of decision making.

There is Risk inherent in almost any activity which has value. Gaining the biscuits required us to cross the road. If we lack the ability to make and assess tradeoffs between Risk scenarios, we are unable to make decisions and gain valuable outcomes. The result is either wild Risk taking and inevitable failure, or doubt and paralysis.

> *I saw myself ... starving to death, because I couldn't make up my mind which of the figs I would choose. I wanted every one of them, but choosing one meant losing all the rest.*
>
> **Sylvia Plath, The Bell Jar**

It is vital to realise this approach is not intended to prevent us from taking Risks but to enable Risk taking. There are several reasons for formalising Risk Management rather than leaving it, as with the road crossing, as a "gut feel" activity.

Collaboration. Walking to the shops was an individual activity. If you are working with a team, you want to share and discuss Risk Management. As with any planning, the team needs to be integrated into the approach. You then need a common approach and language which you can use with your team.

Consistency. Choosing which way to cross the road is very subjective. By making more consistent decisions about Risk you can maximise the value to the business. Making Risk Analysis more consistent allows you to focus attention and effort where the value lies.

Compliance. Buying biscuits uses your own money and is a fairly small investment. Your project choices will have a wider effect on others. Formalizing the approach allows you to demonstrate that you are taking due care with the project and with the resources entrusted to you.

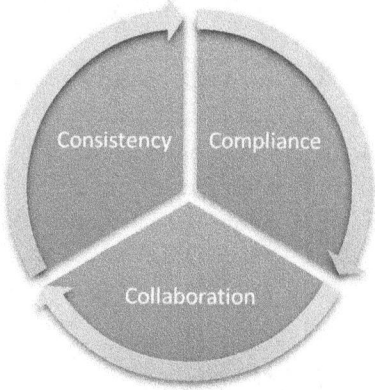

Figure 2 – Why formalise Risk Management?

Discussing Risk is difficult

Introducing more formal Risk Management can be a challenge. This is despite the fact that everyone may be assessing Risk informally. Most project teams and most managers have developed the tools to understand and visualise task-based planning. Schedule and cost are taught at an early age with children learning about calendars and money. But Risk is very difficult for people to understand, discuss and to share understanding.

Think of the project that you are working on at the moment.
How would you explain "how much" Risk there is on your project?
What units would you use to measure the Risk?
How would you explain the difference between a "high Risk" project and a "low Risk" project?

There is a balance involved in Risk Management. In order to manage Risk, you will need to take actions. These actions can and will cost money, whether hard cash or people's expensive time. But any gain is invisible and hypothetical – a future event is less likely, or less serious. So you are asking for real money for invisible benefit. That is a hard sell. Think back to the "road crossing" example. How much delay is acceptable against how much risk of injury? Isn't it easy to say "just take the fastest route and hope it all goes alright"?

> Risk is invisible.

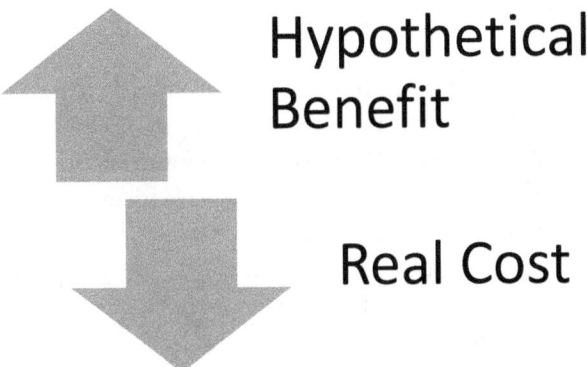

Hypothetical Benefit

Real Cost

Figure 3 - The challenge of selling Risk Management

How can you make Risk Management easier to adopt? This involves a cultural shift and these are never straightforward. In this case it is mostly about language. A clearly laid out and generally followed approach with a shared language and understanding of how decisions are taken allows the involvement of all in Risk Management. It ceases to be an activity for "experts" and becomes something which is valued and included in the project and business approach as a whole.

> *I have worked with teams where it was always challenging to gain attention for Risk management and the prevention of future problems. This is probably typical of "startup" culture where the focus is on solving the problems of today and worrying less about the possible failures of tomorrow. This was well summed up by a comment from a senior manager in the early days "don't tell me about the Risks; tell me about the Issues". Of course following that path means that all of the ignored Risks are likely to turn into Issues.*

Value-driven Risk Management

Risk Management must give a benefit sufficient to justify the investment of time and money. That's the principle of the "Value-driven" approach. As a result, Risk Management must not be a "defensive" activity, designed to satisfy auditors or to avoid blame. Project teams must feel they are managing Risk because it helps them, not because they will be in trouble if they don't follow some process. The belief of teams in the benefit of process is a fundamental part of effective, value-driven projects.

> *Drive out fear*
>
> *Deming's 14 points for total quality management*

It is also important to emphasise that managing Risk doesn't mean being Risk-averse. It is easy to see Risk management as very negative and always looking for problems. But avoiding Risk will typically not maximise value to the business. Instead, Risks are managed to allow risky projects to be undertaken with lower chance of failure.

> *The real reason we need to do risk management is not to avoid risks, but to enable aggressive risk-taking*
>
> *Tom DeMarco,*
> *"Risk Management for Software Projects"*

The overall value of the Risk Management activity is in ensuring that the team can commit despite the presence of Risks.

> Risk Management is about maintaining a reasonable degree of confidence that project objectives will be achieved successfully

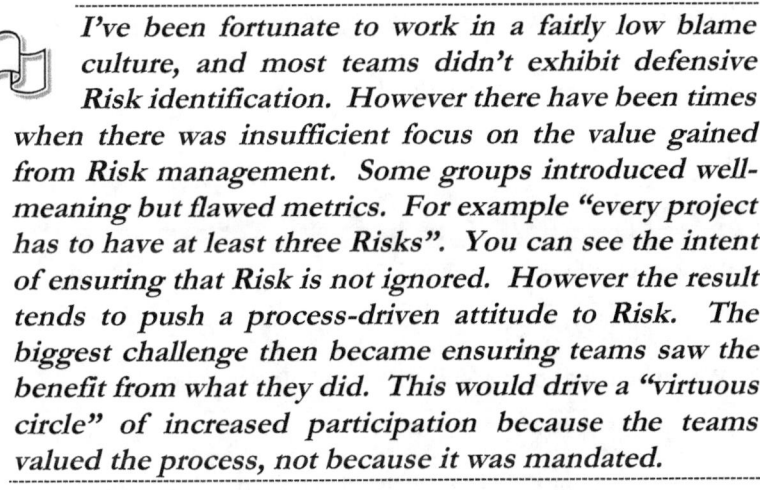

I've been fortunate to work in a fairly low blame culture, and most teams didn't exhibit defensive Risk identification. However there have been times when there was insufficient focus on the value gained from Risk management. Some groups introduced well-meaning but flawed metrics. For example "every project has to have at least three Risks". You can see the intent of ensuring that Risk is not ignored. However the result tends to push a process-driven attitude to Risk. The biggest challenge then became ensuring teams saw the benefit from what they did. This would drive a "virtuous circle" of increased participation because the teams valued the process, not because it was mandated.

Chapter 2 Exercise

Think about how well your organisation manages Risk. Take the opportunity to discuss this with colleagues. And think how well you personally manage Risk on your projects. This isn't intended to be an inquisition, but an opportunity to consider the current status. It is easy to believe that Risk Management is working because something is getting done and a process is being followed.

Below there are a set of questions about project Risk. Have a look at these and see how you would answer for your projects. In each case the "headline" question is fairly straightforward, but think about the sub-questions, which may be a little harder to answer.

Overall, how well in control of Risk do you think that your projects or your organization are?

Do you know your project's key Risks?
- How many other people know? The team? The stakeholders?

When did you last review the project Risks?
- With whom did you review? The team? The stakeholders?

How many Issues on the project did you predict?
- When something didn't follow the plan had you anticipated it?
- What percentage would you say you have predicted?

How many Risks do you manage?
- What do you do to manage them?
- Is it getting value for the time taken?

What is your single most important Risk?
- And if it is important, what are you doing about it?
- How much of your time does it take?

Figure 4 – Risk Process Questions

Case Study – Columbia

Space Shuttle Columbia

The Space Shuttle Columbia was the first shuttle in space in 1981. It flew successfully for many years. On its 28th mission into space, in 2003, the shuttle was destroyed on re-entry and all on board were lost.

This appears initially to be a technology failure – the shuttle was an extremely complex machine and it is easy to view the failure of technology projects as being "unavoidable" events which happen occasionally. So why am I using it here as a case study for Risk?

What happened?

The facts of the loss of the Columbia are well known. Shortly after launch, a large piece of insulating foam used to protect the shuttle from the heat from atmospheric friction, came off and struck the wing. This caused a breach in the leading edge of the wing. Although there was no immediate effect, this was sufficient to destroy the craft on re-entry. Again, this looks like a "technology" cause and not a Risk one. So let's look a little deeper.

Why did this happen?

The Columbia Accident Investigation Report made some clear statements about the causes behind the accident. Some of these make uncomfortable reading.

The organizational causes of this accident are rooted in the Space Shuttle Program's history and culture
Little by little, NASA was accepting more and more risk in order to stay on schedule.

Columbia Accident Investigation Report, August 2003

These statements were not new to NASA. Similar comments had been made in past reports. But despite having raised this over several years, the culture wasn't changing. In fact, possibly it was getting worse.

> *The Shuttle Program's ability to manage risk was being eroded by the desire to reduce costs*
>
> **Shuttle Independent Assessment Team, 1999**

Now this was a safety critical environment. We would expect the assessment of Risk to be a key skill. It's worth quoting some of the key statements in the report of where the teams were going wrong. I will come back to these later.

> *Shuttle Program management made erroneous assumptions about the robustness of a system based on prior success*
>
> *Over time, a pattern of ineffective communication has resulted, leaving risks improperly defined, problems unreported, and concerns unexpressed*
>
> *Engineering solutions presented to management should have included a quantifiable range of uncertainty and risk*
>
> **Columbia Accident Investigation Report, August 2003**

What can we learn?

You may or may not be working on a safety critical project like the Shuttle. However, all projects have requirements for specific outcomes to achieve success. The issues raised in the Columbia report are relevant not just for NASA, but for anyone involved in projects. Maybe you can see similarities to your own projects – I know that we could with the teams that I worked with. The key lessons from the report can be summarised as follows, looking beyond the specific technology

Optimism

It is easy to fall into the pattern of assuming things will go well because they haven't yet gone wrong. Bad practice can become accepted. Short cuts can become institutionalized. Good Risk Management cultivates a "what if" attitude to where failures may occur.

Schedule squeeze

The project teams were being asked to come out with ever shorter timescales. This meant that they were being forced to take on more Risk. From "realistic" plans they were moving to higher risk plans. This is incredibly easy to do. If a task will take 4 weeks, then 1 week is ridiculous. But what about 19 days? Can you really justify needing the extra day? And what if you did that to every task – you could save two weeks on a one year project. The risk level is invisible and slowly a team can accept more and more risk without realising.

I was watching a team presenting at a project review and their plan showed they would finish writing the last tests the day before delivery. They said this was no problem because they had time to run the tests overnight and then ship. The obvious question came up – "what if a test failed?". The team had started with two weeks to fix bugs, and every day of slip they had convinced themselves they still had enough time left. Finally they had no time to fix bugs and were praying that there would be none. Through shared optimism they had convinced themselves this was reasonable.

Communication

If you don't talk about Risk, it won't be prioritised and focused on. Teams need to explain what may go wrong, and management need to ask what could go wrong. To fail to do this means there is no true understanding of the plan.

> There should be no occasion when a problem is known with no decision taken of how it should be acted on.

I first came across the Columbia Accident Investigation Report a year or so after the disaster. As I first read through it, some key phrases really resonated. I remember reading "Little by little, NASA was accepting more and more risk in order to stay on schedule" and thinking "yes, that's what we're doing". At the time I was trying to introduce and standardise a language around Uncertainty and confidence levels. There was real resonance in phrases like "Engineering solutions ... should have included a quantifiable range of uncertainty and risk analysis". We had many projects saying "we will deliver on time – just trust us".

Chapter 3

Identifying Risk

What does a Risk look like?

A dictionary definition of the word "Risk" is shown below.

> *Risk: The possibility that something unpleasant or unwelcome will happen*
>
> **Oxford English Dictionary**

This represents normal English usage. This is fairly close to the usage in projects, although a project management definition might be a little more specific:

> *Risk: an uncertain event or set of circumstances that, should it occur, will have an effect on achievement of one or more objectives*
>
> **Association for Project Management**
> **Body of Knowledge 6th Edition**

We can see there are two key factors here. These both need to be present in order to have a Risk on the project.

"Possibility" or "Uncertain" indicates that there is some degree of doubt involved in what will occur.

"Unwelcome" or "Effect" indicates some degree of impact on the project.

We can use these two basic facts about Risk in how we describe a Risk. Risks can be described with two parts. Firstly there is what **may** happen in the future, which is known as the "trigger". This is the **cause** of the project being impacted. The second part is the **effect** on the project. So any Risk can be written in the form below:

There is a Risk | *EVENT* | *will* | *and will* | *EFFECT*
that | | *occur* | *result in* |

> Risks can be described as an event with an uncertain outcome and a resulting effect on the project

Risks and Uncertainty

It is useful to distinguish Risk from Uncertainty. Uncertainty Management was covered in the previous book as a part of planning. By "Uncertainty" we mean a level of underlying variability within the plan. This will always exist. Even though we may know the tasks we cannot know precisely how long they will take. Unlike Risk, with Uncertainty there is an effect but no single event or cause that can be managed. The effect tends to be visible as a high probability of small variance in schedule. Risk by contrast implies discrete individual events with low likelihood but significant impact.

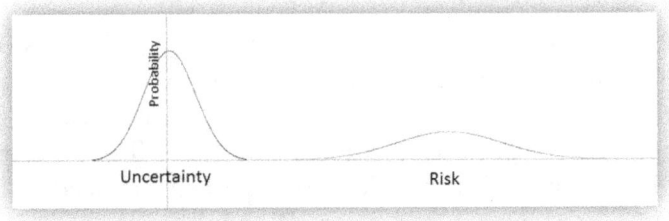

Figure 5 – Uncertainty and Risk

Risks and Issues

It is easy to mis-identify as a Risk an event which has already happened. For example "the project lead has resigned" is not a Risk as it has no associated doubt. The event has occurred. This is referred to as an Issue and needs managing as part of the project execution. There may be doubt over the impact and consequences. There may even be associated Risk due to related uncertain factors (other resignations may follow, the effects of the resignation may be unclear etc), but a past event is not itself a Risk.

Unmanageable Risks

It is easy to get distracted with "Act of God" Risks. Any disaster which might occur to your office (earthquakes, tidal waves, bush fires, meteorite impact) will have an effect on the project, but it is probably not something that your project will be able to manage. Focus on the more probable and manageable events. For example you can identify the risk of icy conditions affecting team availability or making travel hazardous. Or focus on the project impact rather than the cause. What if you lost a supplier (for whatever reason)?

Risks and Opportunities

The dictionary states that Risks are "unwelcome". The Association for Project Management definition refers only to "effect". Within the project management domain, the term "Risk" is often used to include **any** impact on the project, whether good or bad. There's some logic to this, but it can confuse people who are not experienced in the field because of the mismatch with normal English usage. So within this book I will refer to "Risk" as meaning only possible negative outcomes. I use the word "Opportunity" to mean a possible positive outcome. Opportunities then are the possibility things may come out **better** than we had planned.

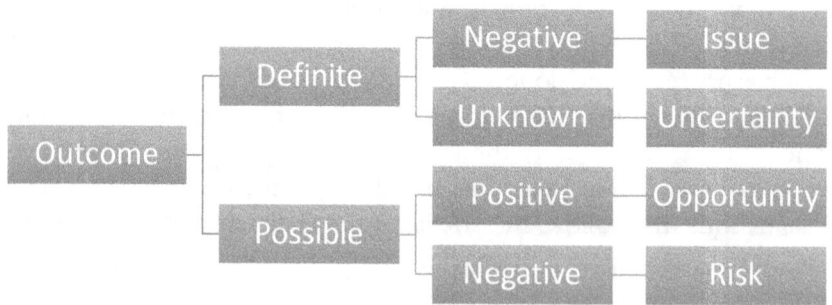

Figure 6 – Issues, Opportunities and Risks

Where to keep Risks

You need a location to store and manage Risks. This is usually referred to as a Risk Register (sometimes "Risk Log"). At its simplest level this is just a list of identified Risks kept in one central place for the project. It could be a document, a tool or a database depending on the approaches being taken. More sophisticated Risk Registers will associate more data with each Risk. Most of that data will be added in the later Risk Analysis. We will look at what we might find at that point, and there is a suggested format for Risks at the end of the book. For now you should be writing down each Risk that you identify, clearly specifying what the trigger event is (what will happen) and what the impact on the project will be (describe this – there is no need to quantify it at this stage). At the least you want to log the event and the effect as you understand them at this point.

For example:

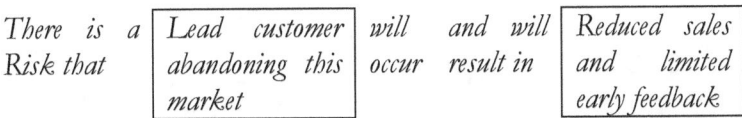

| *There is a Risk that* | *Lead customer abandoning this market* | *will occur* | *and will result in* | *Reduced sales and limited early feedback* |

You cannot necessarily quantify the impact, especially at this stage. However it is important that the causality is visible. We will typically manage the Risk impact by addressing the Risk cause.

When to look for Risks

Before you can manage Risk you need to start by identifying where Risks lie in your project. This means identifying where outcomes are in doubt and may turn out differently from your plan. As you build and develop your plan you are shaping how you expect the future may turn out and you need to be considering where that plan is uncertain. Whenever a new area of planning is performed, the new knowledge introduced will reveal new Risks and may resolve or clarify existing Risks. Start identifying and logging Risks from the start of the project.

In the definition stage of the project you are agreeing what are the project Requirements and how the project will be managed. As you explore what you are being asked to do, and agree what is project success, you will also identify what may impact that success. For example, as the team looks at the stakeholders involved in the project, this may raise areas of Risk (perhaps connected with conflict or differing opinions on how to proceed).

As the planning matures and agreement is gained, some Risks may be closed. You may decide to remove some risky areas from scope. Your investigation may reduce or remove areas of Risk. However, the investigation will also raise new areas of Risk as a potential problem becomes apparent.

You usually expect the key areas of Risk to be apparent by the time you are ready to start implementation. However during the implementation stage we need to watch for new Risks appearing, as described later under Emergent Risk.

How to look for Risks

It can be very hard for a project team to identify Risks. As we have discussed earlier, it may be hard for them even to discuss Risk. You cannot in general sit your team in front of a blank whiteboard and say "tell me all the Risks".

Think about how you have identified Risks in the past. Both when you are managing a team, and as an individual thinking what might go wrong. What approaches have been successful in generating ideas? What barriers have there been?

Even with an experienced team, and even more so with a team less used to Risk identification, it is important to lead the team and "look in the corners" to see what unexpected Risks may be lurking. There are a set of tools which have proven effective in Risk Identification and these are described below

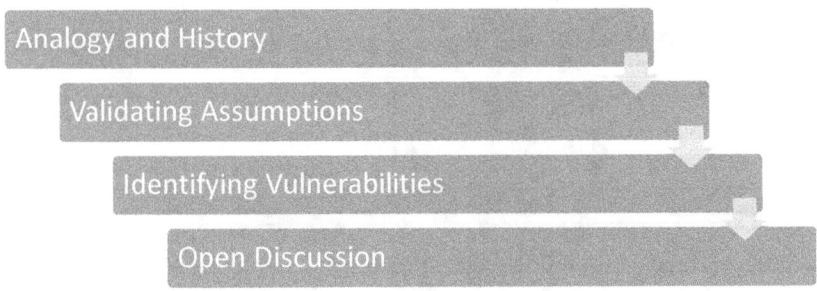

Figure 7 – Risk identification techniques

Remember that you are looking for Risks, not solving them. In my experience with Risk identification one of the biggest problems is avoiding people getting sidetracked. There's a natural tendency when a Risk is raised to go straight into a discussion about how to address it. For a project Issue, something which is affecting the project now, this may be the right approach. However, for a Risk Identification session it can be a big distraction. And there's also a more insidious problem. In my experience it can be hard for people to switch between finding problems and fixing problems. Risk Identification can benefit from a touch of pessimism, while generating solutions can lead the team to being fired up and optimistic. So moving into a solution mindset can cause them to downplay further Risks.

Analogy and History

Those who cannot remember the past are condemned to repeat it

George Santayana, *Reason in Common Sense*

When planning every project you should seek to learn from past projects. Nowhere is this more true than in Risk Identification. You are trying to anticipate what **might** happen and so you need broad horizons about experiences on other projects. Ideally it is already built into your project process to capture learnings from past projects. If you have this as a cultural trope then you are likely to be well prepared for this stage, because you will have a library of past project information to look at. Otherwise you have some hard work ahead of you. You need to find what data you can about past projects, compare projects that are similar to yours and look for themes. Ideally get some of the team from a past project to come and talk to your team, or to present on what went well or badly on their project. An active discussion with the new project team (who will be pretty focussed on this) may tease out a lot more meaning than the old team just documenting issues at the end of the project.

You are looking to gain insight. You may gain the information from data mining, from a "lessons learned" library or from discussions. What are you looking for is to understand what might happen on this project based on what did happen on the previous project. So where are the clues which can help you in this detective work?

The first place to look is the Risk Register for the past project. This will give an insight into how Risks were perceived on the project and what areas the past project team felt were possible Risks. The Risk Register will show what was identified as an area of Risk by the previous team, and you can examine these and consider if they are possible Risk areas on your current project. There is the advantage that the previous Risk Register has been maintained and developed over the whole life of the past project so includes Risks which might not otherwise occur to you until later. By looking at the Risk Register and discussing Risks with the team you will build an understanding of what their concerns were when they were running the previous project and how these same concerns may map to your project.

Once you've considered what each previous project saw as Risks, now move on to what actually happened on those projects. Did anything go wrong on the project? What did the team see as the key Issues during the project? Again, talk to the team or refer to what they wrote during the life of the project. You may need to push a little to understand the underlying cause – the exact symptoms may be specific to the old project but there may be a reason, perhaps an issue in the planning or in the approach taken which might cause a similar Issue on your project. If there **might** be a similar ***Issue*** on your project then you have the two conditions of a Risk – randomness and impact.

The third area to consider is how the items that you have identified were managed Where you have seen there were issues in the past project, were they identified in advance and picked up as possible Risks? Either way, you have some questions to ask. If the Issues were unexpected, then why didn't anyone see them coming? A hard-to-predict Issue is a real area of concern for your project – could there be related Risks that you will also find hard to see? Alternatively, if an Issue was predicted as a Risk, there is still some concern – why did it still happen? What went wrong in the management of the Risk that caused it to occur even though it had been anticipated?

So looking at the history of similar projects in the company gives you three areas of investigation as below.

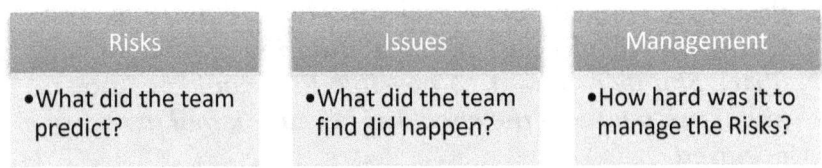

Figure 8 – Historical areas to investigate

Historical data will not tell you everything that you need. In particular, if you focus only on the issues *observed* in past projects, you are poorly protected against low likelihood Risks. These may not yet have been observed because there have not been enough test cases. This point was a key item highlighted in the Columbia report. The report noted that foam impact has been observed and was not intended, and that the fact that it had not yet caused a problem did not mean that it was demonstrably safe.

> *Shuttle Program management made erroneous assumptions about the robustness of a system based on prior success rather than on dependable data and rigorous testing*
>
> **Columbia Accident Investigation Report, August 2003**

I have seen groups with a fair organisational learning culture but no strong Risk based culture. These had a strong cultural focus on learning from Issues, so when a failure occurred it would be fed back into anticipatory checks. This gave a good feedback system to prevent the recurrence of issues. However, by not building this into the Risk process, teams rarely explored the possibilities for related problems. Since the overall number of projects was small, they could end up in a situation similar to the Space Shuttle program. A possible Risk could be known about but not be in the checklist because it had never yet occurred.

Validating Assumptions

The second key approach for identifying Risks is to look at the planning process itself. When you are building a plan, you are trying to anticipate future events. There will be a chain of events in the project – since you are building one plan, you are assuming a specific sequence of events and outcomes. This individual joins the project at this date with these skills, this customer agrees a contract by this date, that material will be enough to hold the bridge up. Any plan includes a set of working assumptions. How are you going to manage these? I've seen planning approaches where "Assumptions" are seen as a separate category along with Risks and Issues, as though you can say "I have assumed this in my planning and if it's wrong it's not my fault". This doesn't seem a great approach to delivering reliable and effective plans. So how can we build the assumptions we are making into a more formal approach as part of Risk identification?

Imagine your plan as a "tree" of possible events. At each event you are making an assumption of the outcome. And the sequence of assumed events represents your predicted future – your plan. So what will happen if an event turns out differently from how you expected? You will end up on a different path. In the diagram below, a different outcome at X leads you down the dotted route to result B rather than result A.

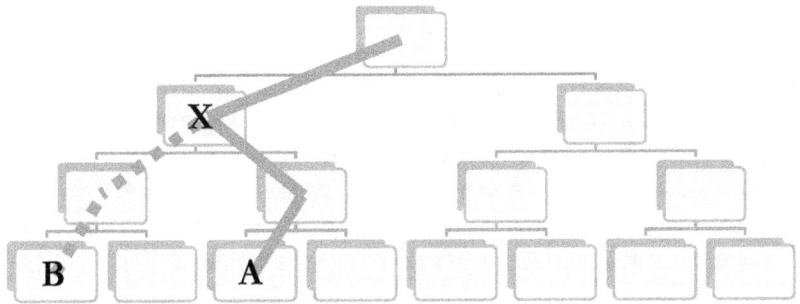

Figure 9 – The tree of events and assumptions

Under this model, **every** event in the future of the project involves an assumed outcome and there is an associated Risk that the assumption will be false, the outcome will be different, and there will therefore be a different result to the project. Again, the two factors of chance and impact are present which indicate a Risk.

 *Let us look again at the "road crossing" example. Your child was heading to the local store to buy your favourite biscuits. They had to decide whether to cross the road or use a footbridge. But what if when they get to the shop, it is out of stock of those particular biscuits? So far we had been focussed on how they got there and had assumed the biscuits would be present. But if they are not, they will now have a long walk to the next shop (a schedule slip) or have to manage with different biscuits (a requirements change). So the assumption leads to a Risk. If you anticipated the Risk there could be an agreed response. If not, the child may have to return home to discuss a new plan.*

We often find that our Assumptions are hidden. That is true in this case. When we put a plan together about *how* to get to the shop, we didn't realise that we had made an assumption about the *outcome* of getting there. It is important to ensure that assumptions are identified and visible. This has two sides. As a planner, you need to state each assumption as you make it, so that it's clear and visible exactly what you are expecting. And when plans are reviewed, reviewers need to be looking at assumptions – are they reasonable to assume, and are hidden assumptions being made without being explicitly stated? It's incredibly easy to make assumptions without realising what you have assumed. And whenever you find an assumption you need to consider whether to log the Risk that the assumption is false. In this case we can state that there is a Risk that the biscuits won't be there. Again this has a chance and an impact, which suggests a Risk.

When I was running a project management team, there was a time when I would review every Project Definition (the basic plan description document) which the team put together. That gave me a lot of insight into how the team planned and lots of coaching opportunities as I could sit down and discuss the approaches being taken. I found that if I were reading a Project Definition and trying to understand and assess it, it would take as long to look for assumptions as all the rest of the review. If you're looking at a plausibly-written plan, it's hard to look behind the planning and spot where there are assumptions being made.

Identifying vulnerabilities

What if you pull your team together and sit in front of a blank whiteboard? Maybe you say "let's write down some Risks". You don't get very far unless you have a very experienced team who have done this many times before? You need to offer some guidance and some themes for the team to think about. And this is where thinking about areas of vulnerability can be useful. Categories of Risk to consider are often maintained centrally by the organisation. These reflect areas where Issues have been seen in the past and give a set of focussed topics to think about Risk.

For example you might have a potential vulnerability area of "Key Individuals". You raise this with the team in a discussion.

"Can you think of cases where non-availability of key individuals has been a problem".

Susan brings up a case in her last project where the build system expert went off with a long-term illness, the regression testing broke and a whole set of bugs slipped through causing later delays. Could this affect this project?

Well, you have Bill and Diana working on the build system so they can probably cover for each other, but maybe the release process is more of a vulnerability as really Mike is the only person who can even find those release scripts, let alone run them.

Solutions may suggest themselves, but remember that's not what this is about at this stage. Log this as a possible Risk area and then move on.

An example of categories of vulnerability might be as below. This could clearly be extended and tailored to specific environments.

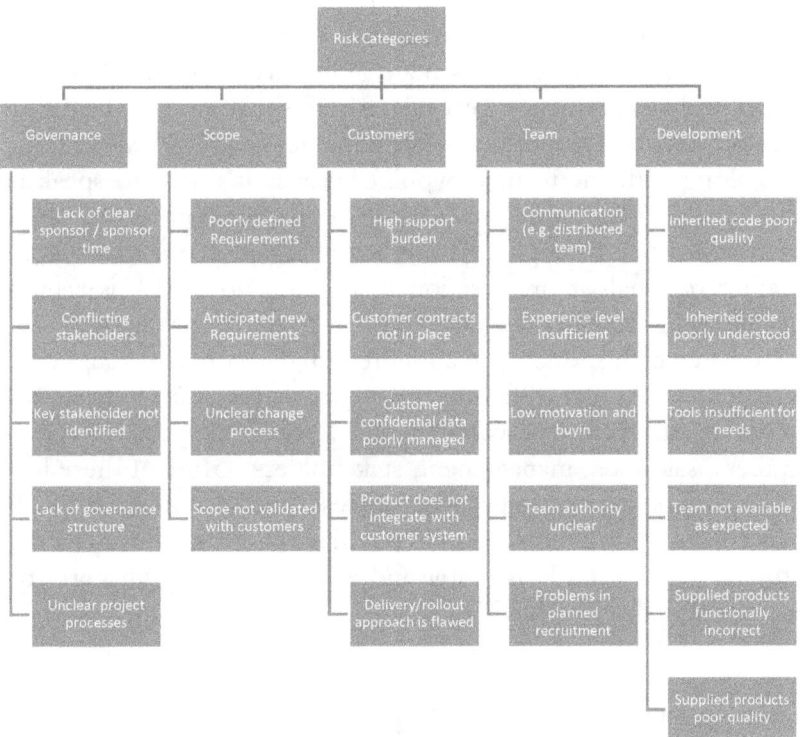

Figure 10 – Categorising vulnerabilities

> *In the project teams with which I worked, a framework of Risk categories was useful in having discussions around Risks. However, the value really increases if this set of categories is well managed. If new Risks flow back into updated Risk categories then every new project has a meaningful level of learning from past projects. Categories then start to merge with Analogy as a means to transfer organisational learning which increases the power of the approach to locate Risks.*

Open Discussion

The final part of Risk identification is having open discussion about possible Risks. This should occur across the team and stakeholders. You want to get everyone's concerns visible and this may be a challenge especially where Risk management is not embedded in the culture. Individuals may be very reluctant to speak up with their ideas. One issue here is "Groupthink" - the tendency of individuals in a team to go along with the team viewpoint because it's hard to speak up against a widely-held opinion. Raising a concern about a plan can be very hard for many people. Also in many organisations and cultures (whether regional or organisational), flagging up a Risk is seen as negative and to be discouraged. You may need to work hard to build a culture in which speaking up about reasonable concern is supported and accepted. As part of fighting Groupthink, you want to make sure you have talked to everyone involved with the project – team members, salesmen, management, stakeholders. Most of these have had no experience of project Risk process, and may find the "Risk" word confusing. Unless you already have a strong business Risk culture, keep the questions simple and focus on asking "what are your concerns about the project?".

Show me the opportunities

Identification of Opportunities is no different in principle to identifying Risks. Remember that Opportunities are "good Risks", where the project may turn out better than expected.

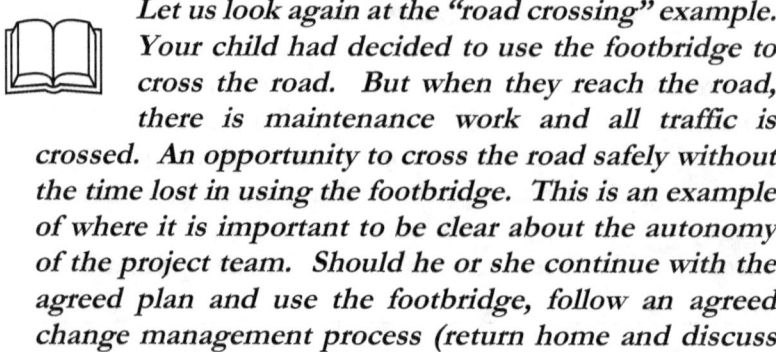 *Let us look again at the "road crossing" example. Your child had decided to use the footbridge to cross the road. But when they reach the road, there is maintenance work and all traffic is crossed. An opportunity to cross the road safely without the time lost in using the footbridge. This is an example of where it is important to be clear about the autonomy of the project team. Should he or she continue with the agreed plan and use the footbridge, follow an agreed change management process (return home and discuss whether to use the footbridge), or cross the road?*

Opportunities need to be as clearly defined as Risks. One area where teams sometimes fail to work well with Opportunities is to be much more vague than with a Risk. It is of little use to say "There is an Opportunity that we may sell more products than we expect". Opportunities, like Risks, should be clearly causal in nature. For example, we may know that a major competitor is considering leaving the market and we can raise an Opportunity to exploit this if it occurs.

There is an Opportunity that	*Our main competitor abandoning this market*	*will occur*	*and will result in*	*Increased customers and sales.*

What is good Risk identification?

You cannot know all of the problems in advance. Even a team that is great at Risk identification will miss something. However teams often underestimate the degree to which they can anticipate many of the Risks. Project failures are often due to reasons that were known about beforehand but not managed or not clearly identified. Sometimes there is a failure of communication, or a cultural barrier, or a lack of experience of how to identify the Risks. Building a consistent Risk identification takes time and effort across the company. To return to the Columbia Case Study, it was clear that NASA had issues in this area. The Risks were known but not communicated or managed.

> *Signals were overlooked, people were silenced, and useful information and dissenting views on technical issues did not surface at higher levels.*
>
> **Columbia Accident Investigation Report**

Risk Identification should ensure that everyone's concerns are heard

In many projects which I have reviewed I would find that everyone knew where the main Risks were in the project. However there was sometimes a huge reluctance to discuss them. In many parts of the business, Risk was seen as "negative". I remember one Engineering Director saying "you can't make a plan for things going wrong, that makes failure look acceptable". It made my jaw drop but he genuinely believed this – he had learned his trade managing crises and had no idea there was a different way to approach this. If you find this in your organisation, it's a hard attitude to work with and takes time and focus to correct. Over the years the teams I worked with became more appreciative of the need for reliable delivery and the tools which would help you achieve this. However, there remained some legacy culture that flagging Risks was negative and viewed as "not being a team player", and this led to a reluctance to speak up. This meant extra work invested in Risk investigation to compensate. One tool which helped was a set of consistent training, ensuring everyone understood what "Identifying Risks" means, and why it is an asset in project delivery.

Chapter 3 Exercise – Your Risks

Try using the suggested tools. Think about your project and where Risk areas might be. Run through the sequence of identification techniques. Or take the opportunity to review another project seeing how the Risks that you identify match those which were recognized by the project team.

- *Analogy and History – what do past projects teach you?*
- *Validating Assumptions – review the planning and look at what you assumed, either openly or hidden.*
- *Identifying Vulnerabilities – use the suggested areas or other categories to think about what might go wrong.*
- *Open Discussion – go around the team and stakeholders and ask open questions about their concerns.*

Identify a few Risks which you can explore further later in the book.
At the end of the book there is a template that you can use for your Risks.

Chapter 4

Assessing Risk

Why should you measure Risk?

At the end of the Risk identification stage you have a a number of possible Risks. These will be in a Risk Register. Quite possibly a large number if you have invested time and effort in the Risk Identification. These Risks are textual and qualitative in nature. You should have some description of the Risk, and you should have identified the trigger which causes this to occur and the way that it will affect the project if it does occur. This is key data, but it is missing an assessment of how serious each Risk may be. If we are able to put some value to how serious is a Risk, then we can make a clear assessment about how much time and effort to invest in addressing it. A well-run Risk Identification will have found too many Risks for you to treat them all equally and intensively so prioritisation is vital.

Risk Assessment allows you to build a prioritisation strategy

How do you measure Risk?

We have said that a Risk includes a degree of doubt and an effect on the project. So when you are trying to quantify Risks, the starting point is to try and put values on these two factors. They are independent factors, which is to say that an individual Risk can be high or low on either one. We call the two factors "Likelihood" and "Impact", which are widely used terms (although other terms such as "Probability" and "Magnitude" are in use, along with many others). Unfortunately neither of these factors will be neat numerical figures. Anyone who hopes to see a Risk quantified as "14% chance of incurring $23,000 cost" is going to be badly disappointed. This is why I favour the word "Likelihood" over "Probability", as high school mathematics seems to have taught people to expect "Probability" to be shown as a numerical value between 0 and 1.

The quote below shows this issue very clearly. It comes from Feynman's writings on the Challenger accident (some years earlier than Columbia).

> *There are enormous differences of opinion as to the probability of a failure with loss of vehicle and of human life.*
> *Estimates range from roughly 1 in 100 to 1 in 100,000.*
>
> ***Appendix to the Rogers Commission Report***
> ***on the Space Shuttle Challenger Accident***

It is not so much that there was a huge discrepancy in estimates that is startling. The surprise is that we cannot look at those numbers and say which is right. This wouldn't be the case with a physical quantity. A space shuttle is 37m long. A factor of a thousand would make it 37mm or 37km. Either would be obviously ridiculous for an object of this type. But a factor of a thousand in likelihood is just a discussion point with no visibly correct answer. Again, the invisibility of Risk and our lack of training in visualizing probability causes a problem here.

What are we are looking for in Risk assessment? The key is enough measurement to inform our decision-making process about how to respond. It should be sufficient to have categorical data, in other words to group the two factors into "levels". We could, for example, rate "Likelihood" and "Impact" as "high", "medium" and "low". There is no specific number of levels which is globally agreed as "best". Simple Risk systems are often portrayed with three levels, and more complex and mature systems typically increase this. Assuming that you are not already using a mature Risk environment which requires a specific number of levels, I suggest as a starting point that three levels gives too little flexibility and that four is a good number.

My own experience with teams performing Risk Assessments suggests that when a three level system was used, there is a very strong tendency to rate most of the Risks in the middle category. This is similar to observations from research into surveys that a middle "neutral" score is overly popular when present (you may have observed that many surveys force you to choose a "slightly agree" or "slightly disagree" alternative however much you feel that you don't mind either way. Adopting a four point scale appeared to generate more thought and discussion and a wider distribution of Risk scores.

Likelihood – will it even happen?

You need to rate the probability of each Risk. As above I would suggest a four level scale. Let's use the arbitrary levels below:

Very High	
High	
Medium	
Low	

We want as much consistency between projects as possible. To achieve this we need to put in place some cross-project agreed meanings for these categories. We could relate them to numerical probability values, but what would these mean? Each project is unique and cannot be re-run a hundred times to see which Risks occur and so to derive evidence-based probability data. Nor do you typically have a large data set of truly identical past projects from which to assess data. You may typically have a small number of similar or related projects with which you are comparing and from which you are gaining historical data. So, let us imagine that we have a small set of perhaps five comparable projects. These would be historic if possible and hypothetical if necessary. Now ask yourself in how many of these the Risk did (or would) occur. You can then apply the loose meanings below.

Very High	The Risk is almost certain to occur unless some action is taken.
High	The Risk has been seen on half of the projects or more
Medium	The Risk has been observed to occur on one or two projects
Low	The Risk has not been observed on a real project but remains a theoretical possibility.

If you are performing an initial Risk identification, you would not expect to raise a Risk in the "very high" category. Having a Risk which is almost certain to occur suggests you have a plan which is not very reliable. It is perhaps better to make a plan based on the Risk occurring, and try to exploit the Opportunity that it does not occur.

Impact – how bad will it be?

Measuring impact consistently is perhaps even harder than measuring likelihood. This is because while likelihood is fairly independent of the nature of the project, impact is closely linked to the details of the project. You can work entirely in monetary value and try and assess a "cost" for every Risk, but this can be hard to assess and very subjective. Loss of one customer might be easy to assess, but one feature? A brand name impact to the company? These can be hard to monetise. Again it is probably best to work with categories and again, a four level scale is recommended, although we have found that "Critical" conveys the top category more clearly than the "Very High" used for Likelihood.

Critical	
High	
Medium	
Low	

The top category is the easy one. A "Critical" impact is something that breaks the project. It prevents the stakeholders achieving a large part of the value, hugely increases cost or causes major impact to the company through legal or reputational issues. The other categories will vary by project and organisation but guideline meanings for the Risk Impact categories might be as below. It may be possible to put specific financial values on these but that may be difficult across projects of different type and size. The focus in the table below is at what level in the organization the impact will need to be managed.

Critical	Fails to achieve a significant part of value or causes damage to the company.
High	Exceeds project team contingency budget requiring project board or executive approval
Medium	Uses significant contingency budget from the project team.
Low	Some increase in task level work, manageable at task planning level

How hard can measuring Risk be?

In the Risk Identification section we looked at issues in project and company culture. These may make it difficult for people to identify and discuss Risks. What about the issues around the analysis of Risk? Unfortunately as we are talking about doubtful, possibly random events, we are in the domain of probability and statistics, and this is an area where there is little common understanding and language. All too often, statistics is misappropriated by people with a message, as when you see two political parties "proving" opposing views from the same data. The opinion is already present and the data is used only to validate it.

> *He uses statistics as a drunken man uses lamp posts -*
> *for support rather than illumination*
>
> ***Andrew Lang***

A misunderstanding of probabilities is behind a number of behavioural fallacies. A common one is the enduring popularity of lotteries despite the poor odds.

Picture a room with a hundred people in it. We offer each of them a choice – they can have ten dollars if a coin comes up heads, or they can have twenty dollars if a dice rolls a six. Decide which you would choose if you were one of them. Imagine that half choose each option. Now look at the results. Well, there are maybe eight people in the room who end up with twenty dollars and twenty five people with ten dollars. Clearly those with twenty dollars are the most successful, so (as is traditional in business) we look at how they achieved this. They chose the dice option, so we conclude that the dice choice makes you rich. However, the fifty who bet on the dice made one hundred and sixty dollars between them, and the fifty who bet on the coin made two hundred and fifty dollars.

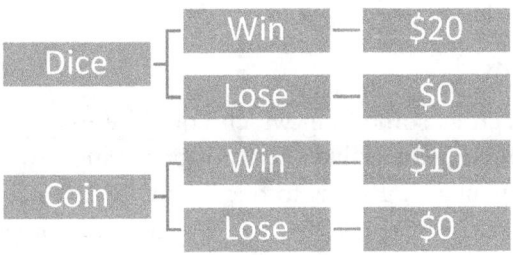

Figure 11- Betting. Coin or dice?

This is a typical example of how observer bias, conscious or unconscious, affects the interpretation of the data. We see it in books looking at the rich and famous – typically they took high risks, and so the book often concludes "risk is good". But of course the sample excludes all the people who took high risks that didn't pay off – we focused on the successes. It's easy to allow bias to affect your judgement of probability. So let's look a little at some of the areas of bias that affect people's assessment of Risk. These will affect the people on your project that are assessing Risk. You should guard against these, as you do against Groupthink, by gaining multiple and balanced opinions from people with varied relationships to the Risks being discussed. Categories here are based on "Assessing Risk Probability" (Hillson + Hulett, 2004)

Familiarity

Evidence suggests that people's familiarity with a topic affects their perception of probabilities. Typically if someone has little knowledge about a topic then this increases their level of caution and makes them perceive Risk probability as higher. Typically this will lead experts to downplay Risk, possibly because they are confident they will be able to deal with it, while novices may either overreact or see something that the more experienced have missed. This is one to be careful about because one's immediate impulse is to ask an expert in the topic being discussed. When estimating an expert may give a low task estimate because they feel the work is easy. Similarly they may give a low Risk probability as they feel that, were they to be doing the work, it would be unlikely to go wrong.

Manageability

If a Risk is seen as something which could be managed, this can be reported as being a lower likelihood of occurring. In theory we are looking at how likely a Risk is to occur **in the absence of us taking any action.** However it seems to be very hard for people to keep these separate when responding. It's almost as though the plan to do something is taken for granted. Of course this is very dangerous, as "manageable" is not the same as "managed". If we say a Risk is unlikely because it *can* be managed then it may be ignored and not actually be effectively managed.

Proximity

It is easy to slip into the pattern of crisis management and focussing on "the next thing". However much we try to focus on anticipation, proximity bias is seeing Risks as more likely if they are close in time and/or space, and as less likely if they are far off. A high-likelihood event in the far future may be downplayed, while a far less likely one which is imminent may be in everyone's minds. This can hugely distort the prioritisation of Risks away from anticipation, which is the objective, and towards crisis management, potentially devaluing the entire Risk process.

Propinquity

People find it very hard to estimate as abstract observers and are affected by their relationship to the Risk. So if the Risk affects them personally then they view it as a higher probability of occurrence than if, for example, exactly the same Risk were in a far-off office affecting people that they don't know. This "self-interest" factor is subconscious, but significant because it can build conflict between a central function (planners, marketing or a project management office) and the project team themselves, with the latter rating Risks as more probable than the former.

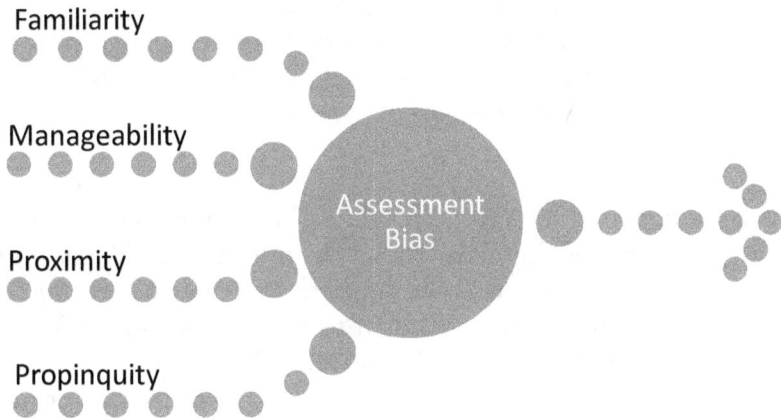

Figure 12 - Risk Assessment bias

Can you visualise exposure?

The overall "severity" of a Risk we call Exposure. This is how much the project is exposed to possible effects from the Risk. It is a combination of the Likelihood and Impact scores. Some approaches try and work with numerical probabilities and impact values, and then multiply the two together to get an exposure "number". This would represent the average loss were you to run the project many times. For example if we have a 10% chance of incurring a $100,000 cost then we could state that there is an exposure of $10,000.

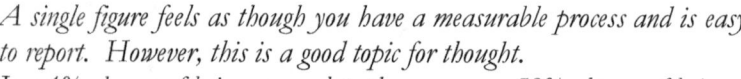

A single figure feels as though you have a measurable process and is easy to report. However, this is a good topic for thought.
Is a 1% chance of being a year late the same as a 50% chance of being a week late? Both would give an "exposure" of 2 or 3 days.
Would you manage them the same way?
Would you report them the same way?

It is good therefore to keep both values. We can visualise the Risks on a two dimensional grid as below. In this grid the Y axis is the Likelihood and the X axis is the Impact. Perhaps unconventially I draw the Impact decreasing from left to right (unlike a graph). This means the first item shown at the top left of the page is the highest Exposure. And rather than have a single calculated "Exposure" number, I have coloured the cells Red, Amber or Green which allows you to "rate" a specific Risk. So for example, a Risk with High Impact and Medium Likelihood would be rated as RED. The medium Likelihood means you have seen similar Risks occur in other projects. The high Impact means that if it occurred it is serious enough that you would need to gain permission from the Project Board to restructure the project, so a RED rating seems appropriate.

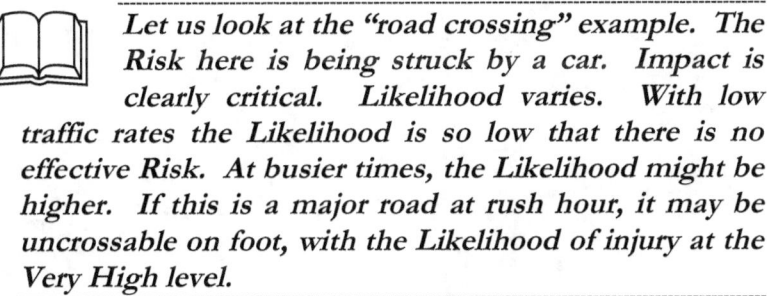

	Impact			
	Critical	High	Medium	Low
Very High	RED	RED	RED	Amber
High	RED	RED	RED	Amber
Medium	RED	RED	Amber	green
Low	RED	Amber	green	green

Figure 13 – Risk Exposure Grid

Let us look at the "road crossing" example. The Risk here is being struck by a car. Impact is clearly critical. Likelihood varies. With low traffic rates the Likelihood is so low that there is no effective Risk. At busier times, the Likelihood might be higher. If this is a major road at rush hour, it may be uncrossable on foot, with the Likelihood of injury at the Very High level.

How good are the Opportunities?

Opportunities can be assessed using the same two dimensions as Risk. How likely is the Opportunity to happen (without assistance)? And how much impact will it have if it does happen? The same scales can be used as for Risks. However you cannot generally plot Opportunities and Risks on the same Exposure table without confusion. For a Risk, a high likelihood, high impact Risk is a problem and is typically shown in RED, while a low likelihood, low impact Risk needs only watching and is typically shown in GREEN. There is no similar accepted coloration for Opportunities. To avoid confusion I would suggest that a low likelihood, low impact Opportunity could again be shown in GREEN, but a high likelihood, high impact Opportunity that needs exploiting needs its own colour, maybe BLUE. The contrast is shown in the diagram below.

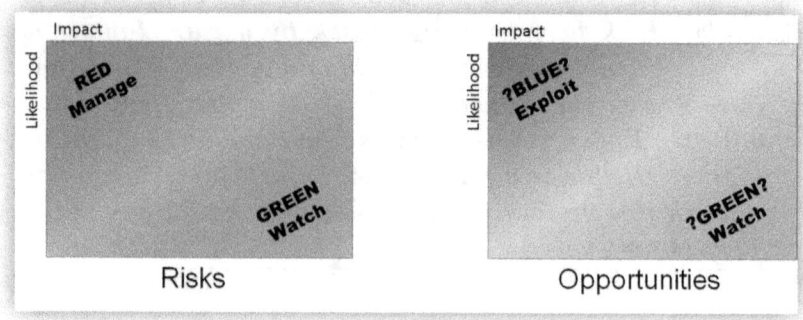

Figure 14 – Exposure for Risks and Opportunities

All or nothing?

In reality Risks are unlikely to be "all or nothing". You may feel that you have a Risk which has a high likelihood of some Impact but the possibility of a much more major Impact. This might be shown in an Exposure grid as below.

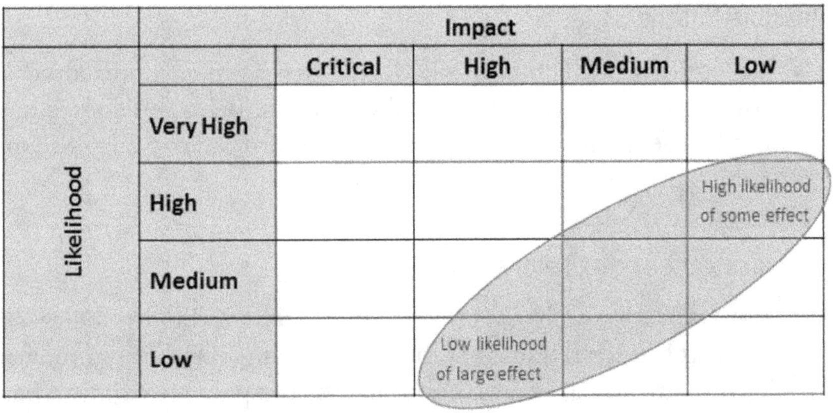

		Impact			
		Critical	High	Medium	Low
Likelihood	**Very High**				
	High				High likelihood of some effect
	Medium				
	Low		Low likelihood of large effect		

Figure 15 – An indeterminate Risk

However, blurring the Risk in this way is likely to cause confusion. The communication and management of the two extremes (high impact, low likelihood and the converse) are likely to be very different. It is best to decide which point concerns you most. This may be one of the extremes, or a point in the middle. If necessary, you can split the Risk into two Risks as below and manage these separately even though the underlying cause is the same.

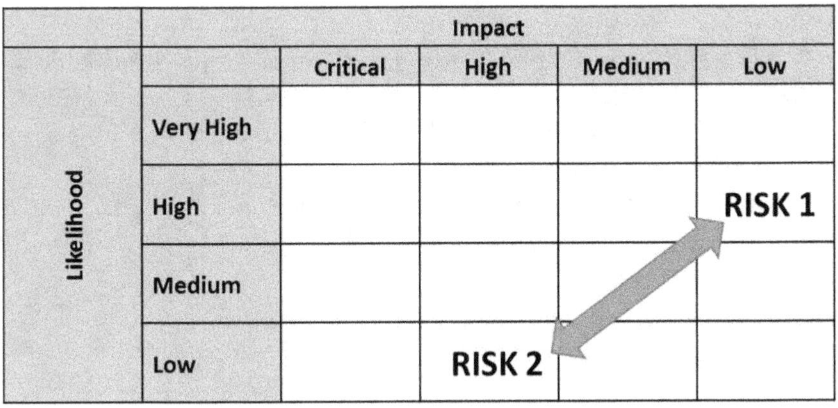

		Impact			
		Critical	High	Medium	Low
Likelihood	**Very High**				
	High				**RISK 1**
	Medium				
	Low		**RISK 2**		

Figure 16 – Two determinate Risks

Chapter 4 Exercise – Example Risks

Let's try assessing some Risks as an exercise. First, let's have a look at a few of my Risks. Where would you put these Risks on the Risk Exposure Grid?

Possible Patent Issue.

The product which you are developing may be covered by a competitor's patent. You are ahead of the field, and so this has not happened in previous products, but if it did for this product you would be unable to ship the product.

New customer brings extra work

If a new customer is introduced there will be an increased support burden requiring some restructuring of task assignments. This seems to happen on about half of the projects of this type.

Lead developer has left

Your lead developer has left the company and there will be a significant delay while you recruit a replacement. You will miss your commitments although not totally prevent the product being developed.

Chapter 4 Exercise – Your Risks

Now think about each of your own Risks which you identified in the previous chapter .

How would you rate these for Likelihood and Impact?

How hard is it to rate them?

Have you identified Risks which cluster in a particular area in the grid, and if so can you think of any reason for this?

Chapter 4 Exercise – Risk Distribution

A group has completed the analysis of Risks across all of their projects. You are reviewing the Risks. The number of Risks in each category is as below. Have a look at how the Risks are distributed across the different categories. Might you have any possible concerns about the spread of Risks that you might wish to discuss with the team?

		Impact			
		Critical	High	Medium	Low
Likelihood	**Very High**	0	1	10	20
	High	0	3	10	30
	Medium	1	10	40	10
	Low	2	4	10	30

Chapter 5

Planning for Risk

Deviation from the plan

Risk represents a possible divergence from the project plan. Risk planning is about managing that possible divergence. So it should always be an addition to good, robust planning for the project itself. Risk planning cannot be used as a substitute for the initial planning exercise or to cover failings in the original planning. Risks will be identified right from the start of the project, before there is a detailed plan for the development. This makes Risk planning a somewhat independent activity to the main planning. However it is closely linked because the planning both exposes new Risk and also resolves known Risk.

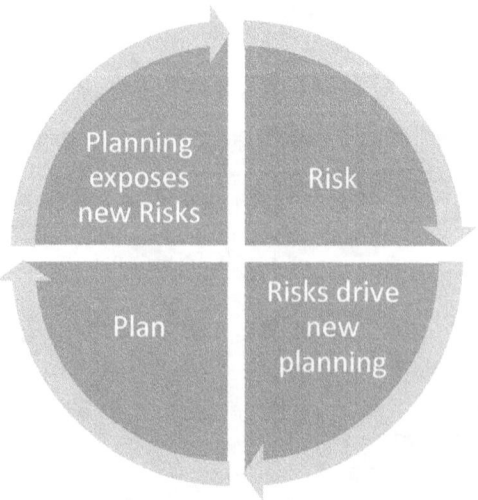

Figure 17 - Risk and Planning

Deciding what really matters

Your Risk Identification may have found a large number of Risks which could affect the project. Quite likely there are more here than you could possibly manage in an effective way. In a Value-driven approach you should make sure you select the most critical Risks for attention to maximise the value from the time you invest. Having assessed the Risks, you can start identifying which you will be managing actively. Typically you will end up with two sets of Risks. One are the Risks that you are prioritising and actively managing. The other set is known as a "Watchlist" – for these Risks you are taking no immediate actions. It is not that these are irrelevant, but that the cost of managing the Risks is less than the value.

> It is better to manage key Risks well than to overload yourself with every conceivable Risk.

You will review the Watchlist periodically. This is to assess if any entries should be promoted to be managed Risks. Typically the distinction between managed Risks and a Watchlist is a tradeoff between level of exposure from the Risk and your capacity to manage Risks. Watchlist Risks are either low Exposure, or can have no active plan until a later point in the project. Use of a Watchlist is an important part of keeping focus on the high value Risks and avoiding excess administration. Depending on the tooling used, the Watchlist could be anything from a separate sheet in an Excel workbook to a filtering switch in an online Risk tool.

> *Our two greatest problems are gravity and paperwork. We can beat gravity, but sometimes the paperwork is overwhelming.*
>
> *Werner von Braun*

Identifying and prioritising the right Risks has been a challenge to many of the project teams with which I have worked. One problem is that the technical experts tend to highlight technical complexity issues as Risks. This is scarcely surprising because it is the area where they are focussed. But because it is where they are focussed, the project planning is already managing much of the Risk in this area. The result tended to be the identification and prioritisation of "easy" Risks, mostly low impact and tending towards the expected uncertainty of the project. An analysis of one group at the time showed that 60% of all Risks being managed were low impact, and less than 5% were high or critical. This was leading to a large amount of effort being spent on formal Risk management of low value items. Over time we managed to shift the balance so that about 20% of actively managed Risks had a high impact or above. Of course the projects weren't inherently risker, but by looking in the right places the teams were spending time on managing important Risks.

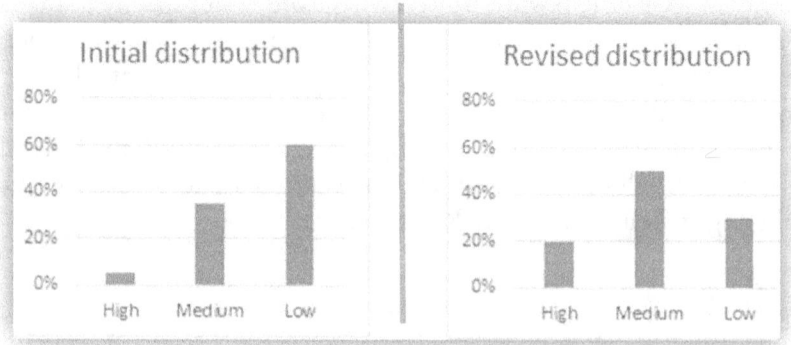

Figure 18 – Shift in Risk focus to increased value

Actions, not words

The idea of a management plan is to reduce either the Likelihood or the Impact of a Risk. Let's look at an example Risk and management plan. The Risk is defined as below:

There is a Risk that a component supplied into the project may be delayed resulting in a delay in delivery from the project.

This is a fairly normal situation with a dependency. We have a cause (component supply), there is some doubt and some impact on the project (delayed project delivery). We have assessed this as medium Impact and medium Likelihood.

		Impact			
		Critical	High	Medium	Low
	Very High				
Likelihood	**High**				
	Medium			Component may be late B	
	Low			A	

Figure 19 – Management plan moving a Risk Exposure

A management plan is intended to shift the Impact or Likelihood to a lower level. Here I have two plans, indicated by the arrows.

Plan A is to maintain regular calls with the component supplier. These will remind the supplier of the critical need to deliver on time, make it more likely that they prioritise my project and so reduce the Likelihood of the Risk occurring. This shifts the Risk downwards on the table.

Plan B is to plan the project so that even if the component does not arrive, the team can make an extra partial delivery while they wait for its arrival. This will not affect the Likelihood but does reduce the Impact on the project, so shifting the Risk to the right.

To be effective, a management plan will affect Likelihood, Impact or both. There are two main types of management plan which can be applied and it's useful to maintain a distinction between these two approaches.

Anticipatory Actions

Anticipatory (or Preventative) Actions are actions which you will take in advance of any possible occurrence of the Risk. They may be intended to reduce the Likelihood of the Risk or the Impact or possibly both. You do not necessarily intend to start on them immediately. Like any activity these are included in your project planning as tasks which need to be completed. They will be part of the project schedule to ensure that they are performed in an appropriate timescale. These activities therefore represent real work and addition to the project cost. This can seem unattractive as they are adding real cost in return for reduced Risk. They do not directly generate project outputs. An example of a Anticipatory Action is Plan A above. This involves time and effort from the project team (regular calls) in order to reduce Risk Likelihood.

Responsive Actions

Responsive (or Limiting) Actions are planned in advance but are only undertaken if the Risk occurs. Plan B above is an example of this. If the component is late, then a partial delivery can be made. This will add project work and cost only if the Risk occurs. Responsive Actions can appear attractive because they have no initial cost. However, they may offer much less possibility for reducing Risk Exposure. Likelihood of course cannot be affected, as the Risk will have occurred. And the options for reducing Impact may be limited after the Risk has occurred.

What is left to worry about?

The management plan for a Risk will modify the Exposure level from that Risk. Likelihood and/or Impact will be reduced, probably into a new category. It may be removed entirely, but this is not generally the case. The remaining level of Risk after the management plan is in place is termed "Residual Risk". This indicates how much Risk there now is on the project, given the plan that we are now following. When reporting project Risk, you should generally report Residual Risk. Your audience is interested in the level of Risk given the plan you will be following. They trust you to execute on that plan, as with the rest of the project plan. In the most Risk-aware organisations you will find that people want both sets of data – initial Risk and Residual Risk. That's because they care about how much they are paying for management plans and want to know they are getting value for money. But the key piece of reporting data is Residual Risk, and we will look later at how to communicate this effectively.

Strategies for managing Risk

What sort of activities do we have as options? We've looked at Anticipatory and Responsive activities, but what can we do to act on a Risk? Here are some of the key approaches which can be used.

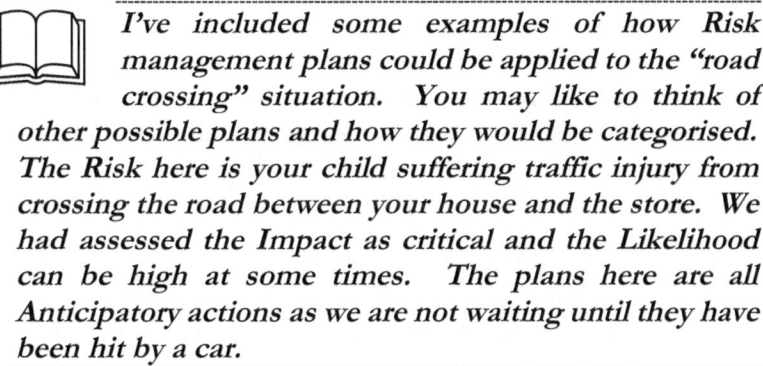 *I've included some examples of how Risk management plans could be applied to the "road crossing" situation. You may like to think of other possible plans and how they would be categorised. The Risk here is your child suffering traffic injury from crossing the road between your house and the store. We had assessed the Impact as critical and the Likelihood can be high at some times. The plans here are all Anticipatory actions as we are not waiting until they have been hit by a car.*

Avoidance

Risk avoidance involves identifying which area in your project is high Risk and not doing that activity. In the example above, we could decide not to use the supplied component in the project, so removing the Risk. Unfortunately projects are rarely so simple. The activities with Risk also often have high project value. The supplied component is probably a necessary part of the project that cannot simply be dropped. But explore this option. If the Risk is too high, you could perhaps make the product without the component.

An Avoidance approach would be finding an alternative to crossing the road. For example if you decided to have some different biscuits which you had at home already, you would avoid the Risk. You are changing the scope to a less attractive solution in order to remove the Risk.

Modification

Modification involves changing the approach to remove or reduce the Risk. In this example, rather than having a supplied component we could develop it ourselves. This would remove the dependency, although add work and possibly Risk of its own.

We developed a plan earlier to use a footbridge. This would be classed as a Modification approach. You have found an alternative way to cross the road which removes the Risk although it involves some compromises (longer travel time).

Mitigation

Mitigation involves doing some activities in advance to reduce Likelihood or Impact. The "Plan A" example above is Risk Mitigation, involving extra meetings to reduce Risk Likelihood.

A Mitigation approach to the road crossing Risk might be to spend some time training your child in road safety. This will be an up-front cost but will reduce the Likelihood of the Risk.

Transfer

Risk Transfer involves moving some or all of the Risk onto another party. An example of this is using insurance to protect you against a Risk. In the example, we might arrange a contract with the supplier which specified a sum to be paid for late delivery. This would transfer some level of Risk onto the supplier (as well as, most probably, increasing Likelihood of delivery).

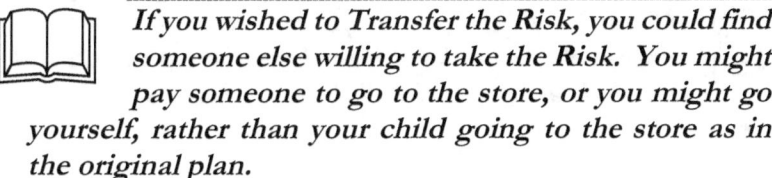

If you wished to Transfer the Risk, you could find someone else willing to take the Risk. You might pay someone to go to the store, or you might go yourself, rather than your child going to the store as in the original plan.

Deferral

Deferral of a Risk involves moving the risky activity later in the project. The "Plan B" example above is a Risk Deferral because it involves an early partial delivery, with the need for the component being (at least potentially) deferred to a later delivery. Typically deferring risky activities allows more time for the risk to be resolved.

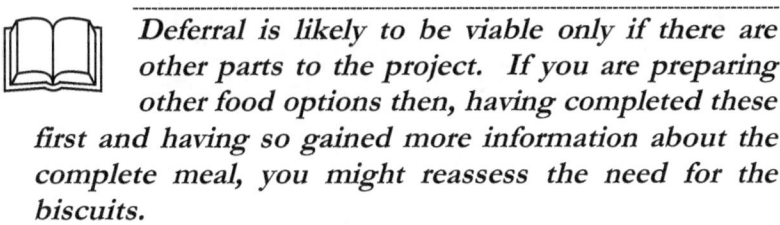

Deferral is likely to be viable only if there are other parts to the project. If you are preparing other food options then, having completed these first and having so gained more information about the complete meal, you might reassess the need for the biscuits.

Anticipation

An alternative strategy can be to move the risky activity earlier. Although that is unlikely to be possible in the case of a dependency as in this example, moving an activity early can give more chance to investigate the task and to respond and replan around what is learned.

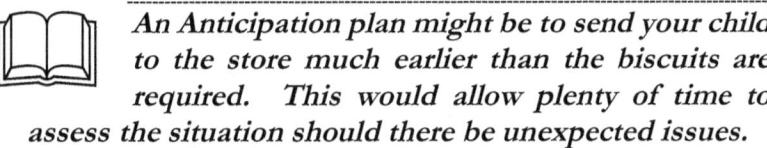

An Anticipation plan might be to send your child to the store much earlier than the biscuits are required. This would allow plenty of time to assess the situation should there be unexpected issues.

Retention

After reviewing the Risk it is always possible to decide no action is needed. This should be a conscious decision that Risk exposure is low enough that the cost of managing the Risk would exceed any possible return. If this strategy is adopted it is important that all stakeholders are aware and approve of the level of Risk being taken on the project.

 *If traffic is light we proposed Retention as the approach. Risk level is so low that no action is needed, although the child can reassess Risk as they get to the road.*

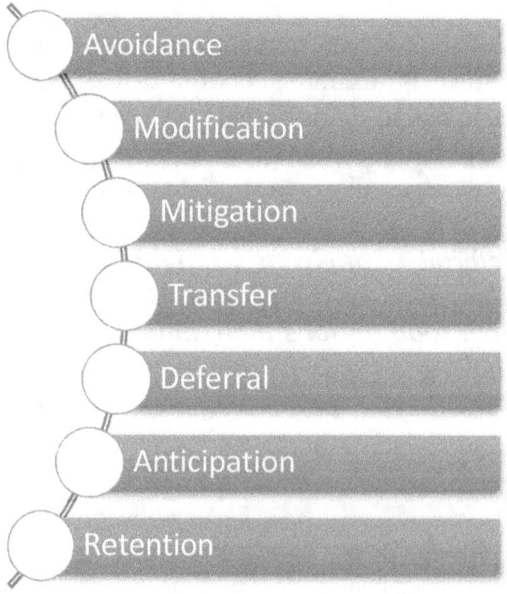

Figure 20 - Risk planning strategies

Risk Management plans

Risk Management plans are managed similarly to other areas of planning. They should be planned out in a similar level of detail. For Anticipatory actions these plans become part of the project plan. So wherever your task list may be, scheduled or otherwise, these actions should be on it. For Responsive actions the actions are filed, typically with the Risk, ready for use if and when needed. They don't become part of the plan as they will probably not be needed. For Risk Management plans, think "SMART". You've probably met this planning acronym, which dates back to the early 1980s, and can be interpreted as below for Risk plans.

Specific	The plan should specify a defined set of activities to execute
Measurable	You should be able to track the implementation of the plan. This will be part of the normal project tracking. Ideally you can also indicate the level of reduction of Risk
Achievable	It is important that the plan is something the project team can perform. There is no value in creating a plan which cannot be delivered.
Realistic	The plan should represent an appropriate level of work for the impact. A Risk Management plan has no value if it costs far more than any possible Impact from the Risk.
Timebounded	The plan needs to be clear when it will be executed. This must be appropriate for the trigger point of the Risk.

Buffering for Risk

In the book on Value-driven Project Planning, I introduced the concept of "buffering". This is a mechanism for stabilising projects of high uncertainty. Here "uncertainty" is the cumulative effect of many small factors leading to an inability accurately to predict the duration of individual tasks. The question then arises of whether the same approach can be used to manage Risk? Could we not add a buffer into a project to protect the project delivery against the occurrence of a Risk?

As a strategy this initially seems promising. Buffers allow you to separate a planned and targeted (unbuffered) date from a committed (buffered) date which protects against a substantial proportion of the uncertainty. In the diagram below the plan date in red has a 50% chance of being achieved, while the committed date in green is much higher, maybe 95%.

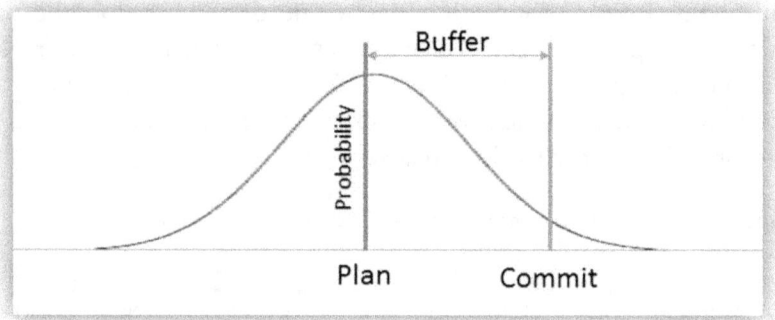

Figure 21 – Buffered date protecting against uncertainty

Would this work for Risks? Unfortunately Risks tend to have a low likelihood but a significant impact, compared to Uncertainty. You are likely to end up with the situation below. Unless the buffer is as great as the possible Impact of the Risk it offers no real protection.

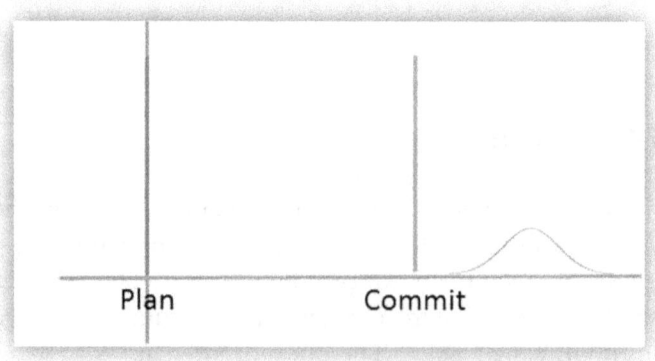

Figure 22 – Buffer failing to protect against Risk

Imagine a Risk which has a 1% chance of adding a year to the project duration. Any buffer of less than a year would fail to protect the project should the Risk occur and would simply increase the milestone dates for no benefit. The chance of being late would remain at 1% and there would be no business value as there would be no increased chance of delivery.

Buffers then are effective for a large number of small factors, and could perhaps be effective for large number of small Risks. But with a smaller number of Risks of lower probability, they would give little assistance. We need directly to manage the individual Risks.

Exploiting Opportunities

A Risk may or may not happen. We use the term "manage" for the actions to make it less likely or less serious. In the same way an Opportunity (or positive Risk) may or may not happen by itself. We use the word "exploit" for actions to make it more likely or more beneficial.

Plans to exploit Opportunities are similar to those to minimise Risk. Anticipatory plans are executed in advance and try to make the Opportunity higher Likelihood or Impact, while Responsive plans are executed if the Opportunity occurs and try and increase the Impact.

Exploiting Opportunities is far less straightforward than it sounds. It is easy to adopt the attitude that you will proceed with the plan, but if an Opportunity "comes knocking" you will exploit it. However, most projects lack the flexibility to exploit Opportunities. This tends to need specific approaches and mindset which we will look at in Chapter 9.

Chapter 5 Exercise – Your Risks

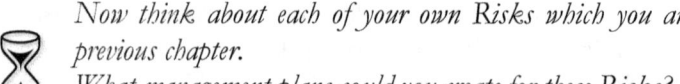

Now think about each of your own Risks which you analysed in the previous chapter.
What management plans could you create for these Risks?
Take some time to think in terms of both types of action:

Anticipatory – *what could you do now to reduce Likelihood or Impact?*
Responsive – *what could you do if the Risk occurred?*

Chapter 5 Exercise – Exploiting Opportunity

Earlier we gave the example of a project Opportunity.

There is an Opportunity that	*Our main competitor abandoning this market*	*will occur*	*and will result in*	*Increased customers and sales.*

Given this Opportunity, how might we exploit this within the project? Think about what difficulties there might be which could be overcome with planning an approach.

Chapter 6

Controlling Risk

Watching for clues

Risk Management is about anticipating and managing deviation from the project plan. So a central expectation is that these deviations will occur, whether through anticipated or unexpected reasons. Tracking project status becomes even more of a high value activity as we realise that the plan is a model and is not expected to be an accurate prediction of the future. We have invested time in producing a good plan, but that doesn't prevent us from expecting that the reality will in some ways be different. There will be uncertainty inherent within the plan and there will be Risks causing unexpected events or event outcomes which lead to changes in the plan.

By tracking the plan we are looking for clues that the reality is not matching the model. We can compare anything that we can measure and have predicted (tasks, measures, billed hours, defect rates, lines of code). Whatever parameter seems appropriate and can be modelled and measured can be used and ideally your plan will track many of these. Of course overrunning tasks can be a problem, but coupled with underbooking on hours this could be a resource availability problem while a rise in support cases might instead suggest the team diverted to other work.

Observing a variance in project status from that expected at this point can be due to one of several factors. Of course, an anticipated Risk may have occurred, so changing the project outcome. Alternatively an unexpected Issue may have occurred which was not on the list of anticipated Risks. Or maybe the deviation is just down to uncertainty and is manageable within the plan structure and buffering.

Regular review cycles

To identify these occurrences you need to institute regular reviewing of the project. Some suggestions on review frequency are below, although this must be tailored according to the length of the project.

Daily

You should be keeping track of project team members concerns and actively looking for problems. This could be by talking to the team or by a more formal "daily standup" process. This is normal project tracking activity, but it is also a key part of managing Risk by watching for early warning signs. What may now be a concern for one individual may be something which could develop and should be managed at this stage.

> *On courses I would suggest the daily cycle of listening to concerns and looking for problems. Most experienced project teams would say "of course, but that's not Risk Management". It's easy to believe that Risk Management is separate from normal activities. Much accepted project good practice exists to address common areas of Risk.*

Weekly

Ensure that the project team get together and discuss Risks. Of course for a large project you cannot get the whole team together, but you should get the leads together, and you should be discussing Risk in such subteams as exist. Getting some focussed time thinking specifically about Risk is important. You should review the status of identified project Risks, look for possible new Risks, look at the progress of management plans and check through the Watchlist to see if any of these are now of greater concern.

> *Regular Risk discussion can be hard to implement. It can require some cultural change to make teams comfortable with discussing real concerns rather than presenting an "in control" face. But it can also be empowering for teams to feel they can express concerns.*

Monthly

It is a good plan to involve your stakeholders in discussing Risks at least monthly. Keeping stakeholder awareness of the level and nature of Risks is important. This is especially critical where you do not have a natural Risk-driven culture. Reporting and giving visibility of Risk is important to ensuring that Risk management gains a good degree of attention.

> *At one point we were running regular formal project reviews monthly. This included presenting and discussing Risks. Initially it was clear that for some project teams there had been little discussion outside this review. The formal review ensured that the team had thought through the Risk status before presenting and that the status had been explained to stakeholders.*

It can also be valuable to get some external Risk review on a regular basis. This could be monthly or at least at project stage transitions. Where possible Risks should be presented and discussed and Risk management plans defended. This level of review gives an opportunity for new Risks to be suggested, concerns to be raised and the robustness of management plans to be challenged.

> *We found external Risk review a very valuable tool. Plans need some level of exploration and challenge to ensure nothing is missed. An experienced reviewer can bring to the discussion what they have learned about both Risk areas and effective plans. Risk coaching is also very effective. Here the project team discuss with a coach what they believe are key Risks, why, and how they will manage them. The coach is not trying to produce answers (and may not be an expert) but to get the team to explore their solutions.*

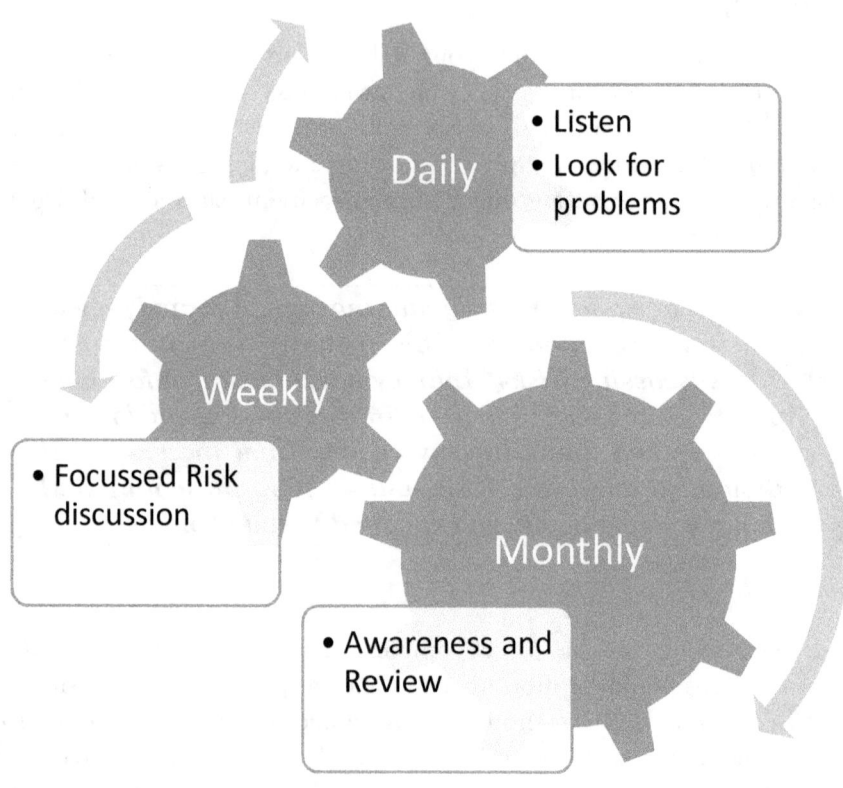

Figure 23 - Risk Control cycles

What are you looking for?

When you are looking at the list of Risks you could be thinking about the points below. You are already progressing a plan to manage the Risk so you are looking for unexpected change, in the same way as with your project plan as a whole. Has there been a change to the Risk itself, or has there been a change to the way that it needs to be managed?

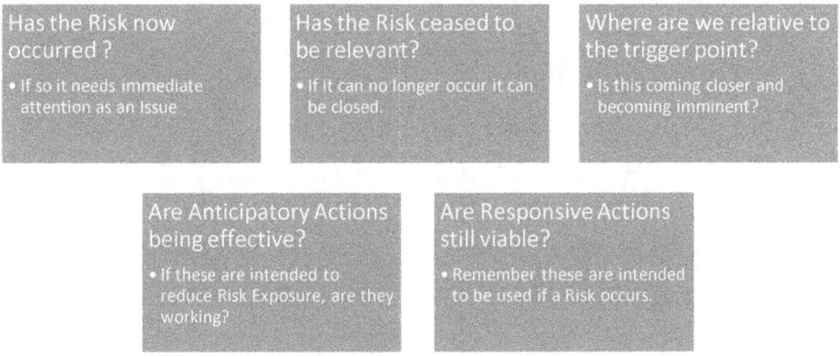

Has the Risk now occurred ?	Has the Risk ceased to be relevant?	Where are we relative to the trigger point?
• If so it needs immediate attention as an Issue	• If it can no longer occur it can be closed.	• Is this coming closer and becoming imminent?

Are Anticipatory Actions being effective?	Are Responsive Actions still viable?
• If these are intended to reduce Risk Exposure, are they working?	• Remember these are intended to be used if a Risk occurs.

Figure 24 – Risk Review checks

Issues - the ones that get away

If Risks are items with doubt and effect, then Issues are effect without doubt. An Issue is some factor which has impacted your plan and has already occurred. Beyond that there is no standard definition of what an Issue actually is, but we can use the definition below from PRINCE2. The main area of lack of consistency between definitions is how serious an event needs to be before it is considered an Issue.

> *A relevant event that has happened, was not planned, and requires management action*
>
> **Managing Successful Projects Using PRINCE2**

It's easy to view Issues as a failure of Risk Management. Surely if an Issue occurs then you have failed to predict and prevent the Risk? Unfortunately that is a misunderstanding of Risk Management. It is important to appreciate what "success" in Risk Management entails.

The intent is not to prevent **any** Issues occurring. You will never anticipate every Risk. Of those that you do anticipate, you will not have a plan that reduces to zero the likelihood of most of the Risks. Most will remain with some possibility of occurrence. And of your management plans, not every one will be executed successfully. As a result, your project remains with a level of Risk which we described above as "Residual Risk".

Issue management is a fundamental part of Risk Management. By accepting the existence of Risks on the project, you accept the need to manage Issues when they arise. Good Risk Management also needs a well-defined Issue Management process. What then are the stages of an Issue Management process when a Risk occurs or a wholly unplanned Issue arises?

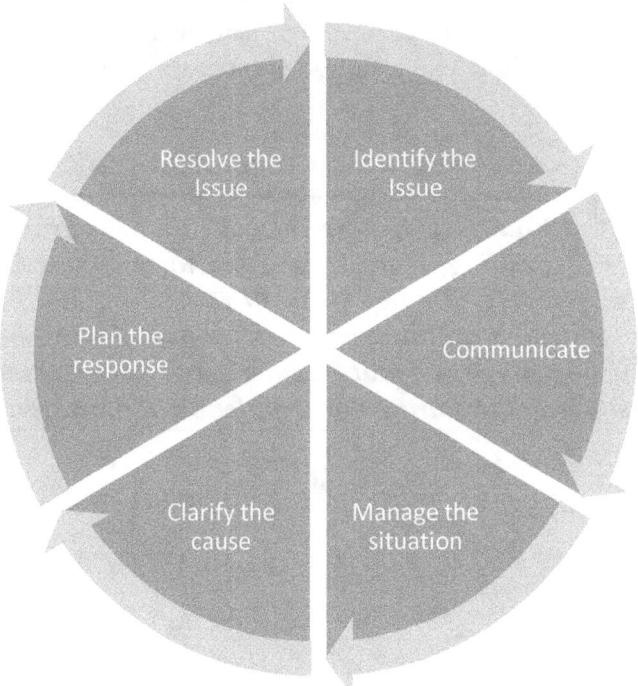

Figure 25 – Issue Management cycle

Identify the Issue

Firstly you must identify that there is an Issue. This will typically require a series of steps. You observe some variance from the expected plan, whether this is a measure or some verbal feedback, perhaps a team member reporting a problem. You investigate to understand what has occurred. It is important to look beyond the symptom and find what is really happening on the project.

The individual reporting the situation may not have the whole picture. You validate that this represents a significant deviation from the plan, beyond the level of task uncertainty which would be expected from normal running of the plan. At this point it is an Issue which will require replanning and potentially will require assistance from your Project Sponsor or Project Board. Now you make an initial estimation of the impact of the Issue on the project. There is a tricky balance here. You want to communicate the Issue as early as possible, but you need something to communicate. You can't wait for every detail, but you also mustn't jump in and panic your stakeholders before you have answers. Make sure you have an idea of the approximate Issue severity and a date when you will have more information before you go ahead and report the Issue.

Let us look again at the "road crossing" example. You have visitors for coffee and your child was heading to the local store to buy your favourite biscuits. He/she had decided to use the footbridge to cross the road. However, when they reach the footbridge it is being repaired and can't be used. Clearly there is an Issue here preventing the completion of the original plan.

Communicate the Issue

By definition the impact of the Issue on the project is significant. Your stakeholders will need and want to be made aware of the Issue as it will have an impact on the project. And this key communication needs to be well managed. Just sending out a broadcast email is very unlikely to be an appropriate way to communicate a project Issue. Stakeholders will understandably be concerned about what has happened and what the effect will be. Your first job is to make sure that they have a clear understanding of impact and status. This usually means individual communication or a clear group presentation of the Issue, making it clear how serious the Issue is, whether you need help at that point and when you will be able to add more detail. Your Issue reporting needs to cover the three key points below.

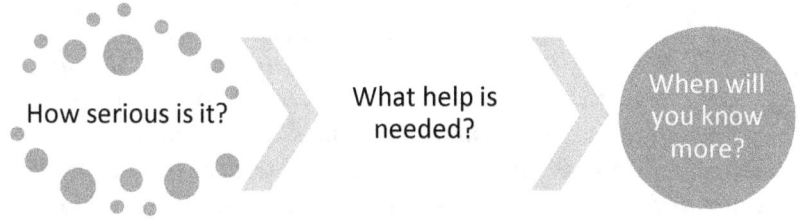

How serious is it? > What help is needed? > When will you know more?

Figure 26 – Messaging Issues

In the "road crossing" example you are the stakeholder. It would be no use your child returning and not informing you that they didn't have the biscuits. That sounds obvious, but many project teams avoid conflict by not communicating bad news. So what is the communication here? The objectives have not been achieved (no biscuits). What help is needed? A new plan needs to be developed to obtain the biscuits. And there can be no progress until the new plan is agreed.

Manage the situation

The initial task is to manage the Issue itself. If you had already anticipated this as a Risk, you may have one or more Responsive Actions planned to execute if the Risk occurs. If so, this is the time to execute them. This is the test of whether you really thought these through and have been maintaining them. It's not unusual to discover that the Responsive Actions that you created at the start of the project are now out of date and rely on people, teams or tools that are no longer available, and Issue resolution is not the time to discover this. If you had not anticipated the Issue, you need to decide what you can do to minimise the impact of the situation.

This is often the one area where project teams focus their time. They respond well to the immediate situation (the crisis) but sometimes neglect the other areas of the Issue management process.

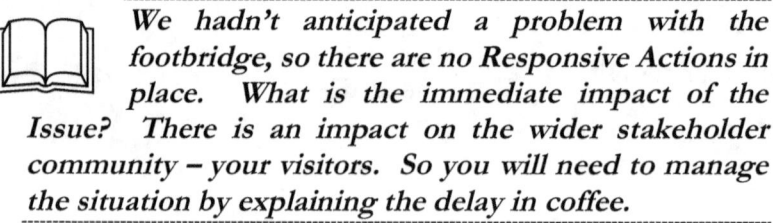

We hadn't anticipated a problem with the footbridge, so there are no Responsive Actions in place. What is the immediate impact of the Issue? There is an impact on the wider stakeholder community – your visitors. So you will need to manage the situation by explaining the delay in coffee.

Clarify the impact

Once you have understood the immediate situation, you need a clearer understanding of the impact on the project. This is the point where you want to be using Root Cause Analysis to understand why the Issue has occurred.

When an Issue is first reported, you will see a symptom – one piece of data or one individual's view. You want to develop a questioning approach. If you ask "why did this happen?" you will find more of the background. Ask "why?" again, maybe several times, and you eventually reach the "Technical Occurrence Root Cause", or an understanding of why this Issue **occurred**. If you understand this you can now develop a plan to fix the Issue and can explain to your stakeholders the underlying facts behind the Issue. By continuing to ask "why?" you can also ascertain the "Technical Escape Root Cause". This is why the failure wasn't **identified** in advance. This is valuable to ensure that you won't have other similar and related Issues on your project. And finally you can determine the "Systemic Occurrence Root Cause" which is the information that could be used to **prevent** other projects having the same Issue. This can be fed into the corporate processes or back into the Risk Vulnerability category data.

> *the basis of Toyota's scientific approach ...*
> *by repeating "why" five times, the nature of the problem*
> *as well as its solution becomes clear*
> *Taiichi Ohno, "Toyota Production System"*

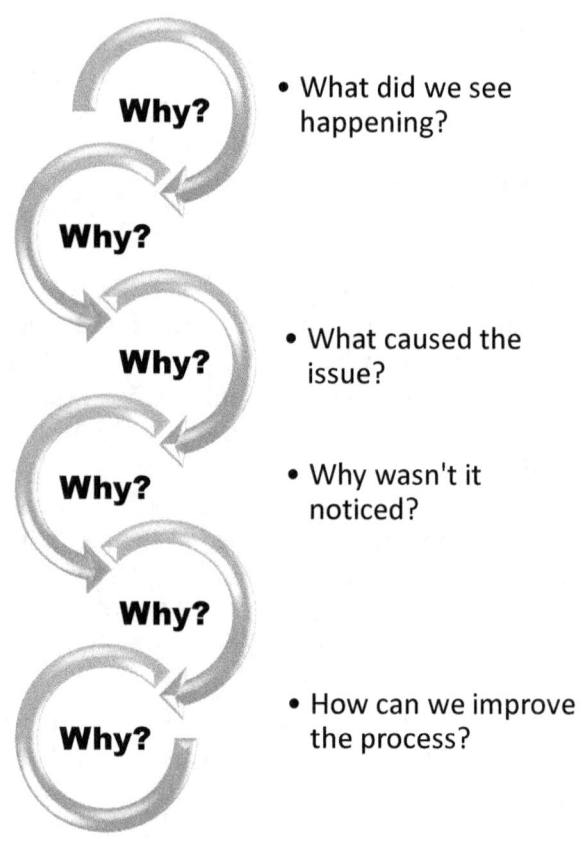

Figure 27 - Asking 5 whys

I discovered the effectiveness of this approach of asking "why?" to push from symptoms to root cause. It takes some practice and confidence, because it's easy to seem annoying and give up, but in my experience keeping nagging away with "why" questions does pay off. The approach is central to the Toyota approach known as "5 whys". The name comes from Toyota's empirical evidence that you probably need to ask "why" at least five times. Once you have the Technical Occurrence Root Cause you can build your plan to fix the project, but make sure you come back and ask more "why?" questions later.

Let's look at how "5 whys" might work in the "road crossing" example.

You discuss what has happened:

[1] **Why** *haven't you got the biscuits?*

I couldn't get to the shop.

[2] **Why** *couldn't you get to the shop?*

I couldn't use the footbridge

[3] **Why** *couldn't you use the footbridge?*

It was blocked

[4] **Why** *was the footbridge blocked?*

I hadn't realised it was being repaired

[5] **Why** *did you come back?*

I wasn't sure if I should cross the road

It is important to manage this in a non-confrontational manner. This is about understanding the problem not blaming the individual. By repeated "why?" questioning we now understand what happened.
Technical Occurrence Root Cause. The problem occurred because the footbridge was blocked
Technical Escape Root Cause. We hadn't known in advance because we lacked the information about the bridge repair schedule
Systemic Root Cause. We could prevent the issue in future by gaining better information and by being clear whether footbridge usage was mandatory.

Plan a new scenario

Issues are dangerous because they invalidate your plan. Once an issue has occurred, some or all of your plan is no longer an accurate representation of what is needed on the project. So you are in the position of no longer having a plan to demonstrate how you will achieve project success. To some degree you are "flying blind". Restoring this is your key priority once the immediate crisis is under control and you understand the TORC and so know what corrective actions to put in place. You need to work with the team and stakeholders on a new plan which integrates the changes which are needed because of the Issue.

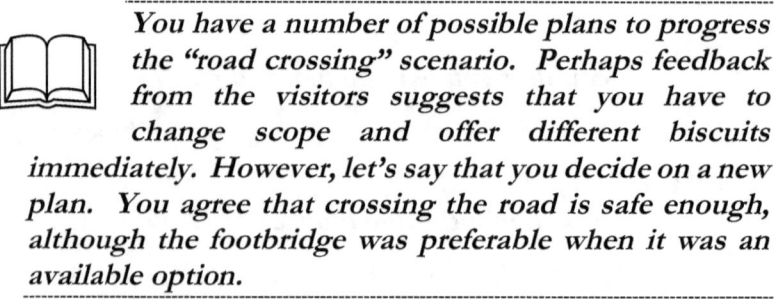

You have a number of possible plans to progress the "road crossing" scenario. Perhaps feedback from the visitors suggests that you have to change scope and offer different biscuits immediately. However, let's say that you decide on a new plan. You agree that crossing the road is safe enough, although the footbridge was preferable when it was an available option.

Resolve the issue

Resolving issues is a misunderstood area. An issue is resolved when you have a plan to deal with it, not when all related actions have been completed. That is why "resolved" is probably a clearer word than "closed". The item only needed be managed as an Issue because it was outside the plan. We want to turn around issue resolution as quickly as we can, because Issues cause alarm and confusion.

Make sure that you replan as quickly as possible and get back to Stakeholders for approval of the new plan. It may not be obvious that they are nervously waiting for the Issue to be resolved, but they are. And make sure you clearly explain that you now have a plan to address the problem, rather than the problem having vanished. You will probably have to continue reporting on the progress of that plan for some time.

In the "road crossing" scenario, the Issue is resolved with the new plan. You have agreed your child will go back and cross the road, and you have agreed with the visitors that the delay is acceptable. At this point the Issue is closed. The biscuits will not be available for some time, but there is an agreed plan to produce them.

Case Study - Issues

Tacoma Narrows Bridge

The first bridge was built at Tacoma Narrows between November 23, 1938, and July 1, 1940. It was, at the time, the longest suspension bridge made.

However, it gained the nickname "Galloping Gertie" after it was found that in high winds it would oscillate up to 2m vertically. People would travel for miles to drive across it.

What happened?

On Nov 7th 1940 the bridge started oscillating more violently and eventually collapsed.

The Tacoma Narrows Bridge cost $6.4M. It lasted only 4 months.

Why did this happen?

The aerodynamic effect of the wind blowing across the bridge caused the bridge to oscillate. In the right conditions the oscillation proved so severe that the bridge collapsed.

Design of the bridge had considered only static loading, as was normal for the time, and had not realized the possible dynamic effects caused by wind action. Subsequent studies assessed the issues and correctly identified the cause, improving the standards for future bridge building.

> *From now on, bridge designers must consider dynamic actions and aerodynamic effects.*
> *Wind tunnels, elastic models ... and studies of aerodynamics, resonance and damping must now take their place in the design of any highly elastic bridge.*
>
> **Pacific Builder and Engineer. December 1940.**

What can we learn?

The Tacoma Narrows bridge is an example of a major Issue and the subsequent learning. No error was made in the planning or construction, but the size and flexibility of the bridge brought into play effects not previously observed. The root cause of the failure was identified, along with the changes that would be needed to prevent further such failures in the future. These changes were successfully put in place in the construction industry.

Although the Tacoma Narrows bridge was a costly failure, it was also an example of successful learning from mistakes.

Chapter 7

Communicating Risk

The first thing to remember about communication is that you are communicating to individuals. Each individual stakeholder will have a different interpretation of the messages that you are communicating. As we discussed earlier in the book, your audience's understanding of Risk may be very varied. Some may have had significant training in Risk management and others may have no previous exposure to the concepts. Some organisations will have very clear language and specific key words will be well understood. Individuals will react differently to different cues.

You should never just report a problem. Always ensure you explain the action that you will take, the help that you are requesting, and the timescale to produce a further response.

Consider the messages below. They may relate to the same Risk, but will generate different responses. Risk messages typically need to be very clear about both status and assistance needed. You need to show where you are in control and where you are asking for help.

"We will probably deliver late"

"We have a Risk that has a significant chance of making the project late"

"We have a Risk that could cause 4 weeks delay. We have a plan to mitigate it. Costs are within the project's contingency budget and Residual Risk is very small."

Risk messages

There are two main Risk messages which you are communicating. One is a message about the project and the project status. How confident are you about the project delivering? How much overall Risk is there on the project? And remember this is Residual Risk. After all that you are doing to manage the project, how confident or concerned should your stakeholders be? All of your stakeholders will be interested in this message. As stakeholders they are necessarily interested in the project delivery and they want to know if they should be worried. At one level this is the typical "are we on track" message, but is more complex because of the doubt involved in Risks.

> **Reports should be focussed on Residual Risk**

The other message is specific to a Risk. What is the Risk? How much should people be concerned about **that specific Risk**? And the audience interest in this will vary. For each Risk some stakeholders will be interested, and some will be less so. Typically a stakeholder is, or should be, aware of a Risk if it is something which they can influence. They will need to stay informed to find if you need their assistance. Also you may need them to stay aware of the Risk because you know that they are needed.

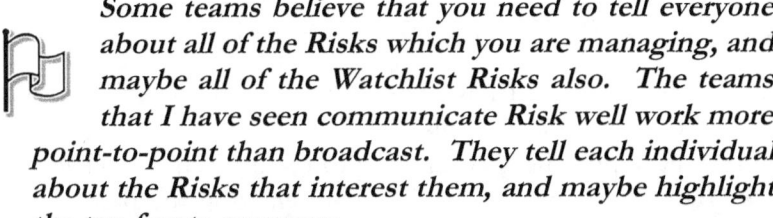

Some teams believe that you need to tell everyone about all of the Risks which you are managing, and maybe all of the Watchlist Risks also. The teams that I have seen communicate Risk well work more point-to-point than broadcast. They tell each individual about the Risks that interest them, and maybe highlight the top few to everyone.

Hearing the message

You need to ensure that the message is not just delivered, but is heard. As we have seen, Risk language can be misunderstood and messages about hypothetical events can be easy to ignore. You may need to get stakeholders to "play back" the message to ensure it has been received. In some cases you may need careful stakeholder management and may need to get support to influence stakeholders to pay attention to Risk messages.

> *Some projects need to take on a high level of Risk. It can be very important to ensure that everyone understands these are not "business as usual". One project team was aiming for very aggressive targets to hit a market opportunity. The stakeholders had agreed this might well fail. There was a plan to manage the situation if delivery was at the later date predicted by the planning. Eventually the team did deliver at the plan date and missed the earlier opportunity date. Because the team had been very careful about messaging, and everyone was agreed about the Risk level, it was clear that this was still "Success".*

Appetite and accepting the message

Different stakeholders will have a different view of how much Risk is acceptable on the project. This will typically be weighted by how much they have personally committed to the project. It will also be affected by how the project has been presented in the past. If the stakeholders believes this to be a stable iteration of a classic product development, they may approach Risk very differently from a project which is presented as innovative. Just as someone discussing investments with you, you need to understand your stakeholders' perception of Risk. This is what is termed "Risk Appetite" – how much Risk are they comfortable to take on? This is very subjective.

An example is the shift in travel patterns after the terror attacks of 2001. Although exact numbers are hard to ascertain, there have been several articles (e.g. Wall Street Journal, March 23, 2004) which examined this. Passenger miles on the main US airlines fell substantially by up to 20%, while road use increased by perhaps 3%. However, it is widely accepted that accident rates per mile from road travel are much higher than from airline travel. The result was an overall increase in fatal travel accidents as a result of trying to avoid fatal accidents. Travellers have a higher appetite for Risk in cars than in air travel and were shifting from a low risk to a higher risk mode of travel.

Why should this be? In his book "Risk", Adams argues that there are two dimensions involved. One of these is about the motivation – you are more willing to take risks if you chose to do the activity. The other is the level of control – you are more willing to take risks if you feel you are in control. So you are more comfortable with a higher level of Risk when driving (where you are in control) than when flying (where you are a passenger). You are more comfortable if you have chosen to travel than if you travel for work. At the two extremes, you are comfortable with a high level of risk when rock climbing because you choose to do it and your own abilities define your safety. You are uncomfortable with a similarly high level of risk of being robbed because it is non-voluntary and not in your control.

Let's map this to a project stakeholder situation. A stakeholder is more comfortable with Risk if he or she feels in control and that he or she chose to do the activity. Clearly therefore stakeholder buy-in is critical to making them comfortable with Risk. You will need to make sure that they are aware of the level of Risk that is being taken and that they have agreed to it. You also need to make sure they feel in control because the Risk is being managed and reported adequately.

Stakeholders need to be comfortable with the level of Risk

Risk Response level

It is worth considering at what level of the organization a Risk needs to be managed and reported. This is separate from which individual stakeholders are interested in specific Risks. Although the Risk may have been discovered at a project level, it typically can be categorized as applying at one of the following organizational levels.

Project Level Risk

These are Risks which are entirely within the project. The project team can manage the Risk without assistance. The impact of the Risk may need a response from outside the project team but those outside the team don't need to plan for a response. In general therefore there needs to be no awareness outside the project team except by individuals interested in the specific Risk. This type of Risk will generally have low Impact, which means that awareness at a more senior level is not needed, and have low complexity and cost Management plans which can be managed as part of the project.

Programme Level Risk

Some Risks will need to be escalated to a Programme level. The Impact could threaten a larger programme, other related projects or a corporate goal towards which this project contributes. The Programme Management Team will need to be aware of the Risk and monitor it within the Programme Risks. The project team may also need budget or influence assistance from the Programme to progress the management plan.

Strategic Level Risk

Risks may need to be escalated to a strategic business level. These are generally Risks which have significant Impact, even if Likelihood is low. Risks that could affect the business (revenue, reputation, legal issues) may need to be reported at a high level. The management plan may also need executive input or support to progress.

Figure 28 – Risk Escalation level

Chapter 7 Exercise – Your Risks

Now think about each of your own Risks which you identified earlier. Who are the key stakeholders for each Risk who need to be kept informed about Risk status?

How would you report the Risks?

At what level should each Risk be managed – Project, Programme or Strategic?

Chapter 8

Risk Management is not enough

Case Study – Eyjafjallajökull

Eyjafjallajökull

In 2010, air traffic over much of Europe was disrupted through much of April in the largest shut-down since the Second World War. Passengers were stranded across Europe and attempting to travel to other countries. Around 100,000 flights were cancelled. The cancellation had been unexpected and unpredicted and caused huge expense and disruption.

What happened?

The events were caused by a volcanic eruption under the Eyjafjallajökull ice cap on Iceland. As well as local damage, the eruption threw volcanic ash high into the atmosphere. Airborne ash was known to be hazardous to aircraft and aviation authorities responded with a flight ban.

Why did this happen?

The eruption was an unpredictable event which could not specifically have been identified by Risk Management. There was minimal warning of an eruption and no indication that one at this location would have significant global impact.

What can we learn?

Many key individuals for projects were stranded at remote locations. I recall many of my colleagues being unable to return home. This is an impactful event which cannot be predicted or directly be managed as a Risk. But that doesn't mean that such events can be ignored. What if your project were impacted? There are two areas where we can apply Risk management, even though the event itself could not be predicted.

When an event such as the Eyjafjallajökull eruption occurs, it changes the parameters for the project. It is important to re-evaluate Risk in the new environment. How does the non-availability of key individuals, perhaps for two weeks, raise new Risk areas? What management plans could be put in place?

The second key point is to learn from the event and make projects more robust against similar events. Although the exact event cannot be predicted, the impact of a class of events can be anticipated. Organisations have learned from this event and fed it back into the database of vulnerabilities for future projects. Whether due to a similar volcanic situation or another effect (such as terrorist attack) projects could consider the imposed suspension of air travel for several days, leaving key individuals in different locations.

What is Emergent Risk?

At the start of the book we talked about Risk as being about "known unknowns". In order to identify and assess Risk you need to be aware of what might happen on the project and where it may not follow your plan. When we looked at the methods used to identify Risk they are all based on knowledge, whether from past history or from learnings in the planning process. But what about the "unknown unknowns"? These are the areas that could not possibly be predicted at the start of the project. Just to repeat for clarity, these are not "low Likelihood" Risks, or ones that will need some investigation to find.

There are possibilities for your project to go wrong that you cannot know at the start of the project. This shouldn't really be a surprise. The planning process gains more information, and this learning continues through the project. As you learn you may become aware of new areas of Risk. And the external environment around the project changes over time. New stakeholders and customers are introduced, standards, interfaces and regulatory frameworks change, business needs are modified. These cannot necessarily be predicted at the start of the project.

What can you do? Don't throw your hands up and say that if you can't see everything at the start, you won't bother with Risk Management. Identifying Risks is never easy, but for the bulk of Risks it is possible to think about and plan for the bulk of the Risks on the project. The approach we have described here is very effective for most Risks but it is not sufficient for all Risks.

Rare as a black swan

In his book "The black swan: the impact of the highly improbable", Taleb refers to these type of Risks as "Black Swans". This rather catchy name has become quite widely adopted to represent Emergent Risks. The name derives from the expression "As rare as a Black Swan". This was originally a Latin expression to represent something impossible.

> *rara avis in terris nigroque simillima cygno*
> *a rare bird in the lands, very much like a black swan*
>
> **Juvenal**

The phrase became popular in Europe in the 16th century in rather the way we might talk about "Pink Elephants". European swan species, after all, are uniformly white and so there was the mind-set that swans were, and had to be, white. However, when Europeans reached Australia they discovered *Cygnus atratus*, the southern hemisphere swan, which is primarily black. The reasonable assumption that swans were necessarily white had to be abandoned and the expression, understandably, stopped being used and has largely been forgotten.

Central to the "Black Swan" concept for Risks is that no past data can point to the possibility of occurrence of a Risk of this type. It cannot therefore be a "known unknown" because no relevant knowledge exists. As a result it cannot be identified as a Risk using any conventional means. There simply was no evidence to suggest that black swans might exist (and a mountain of evidence to the contrary). A worse problem still is that these "black swan" Risks are often serious in impact. Because they represent a paradigm shift in the project nature and assumptions, they can have a huge, maybe catastrophic effect on the project.

The Risks are termed "Emergent" because they become revealed by changes in circumstances. In the case of the swans, the addition of data from Australia indicated the possibility of black swans. In the Eyjafjallajökull eruption the assumption of free travel of individuals was shown to be unreliable. More generally for an emergent Risk there is a change in external circumstances which introduces or reveals some entirely new factor of which the team was not previously aware. This gives us a clue about how to manage Emergent Risk.

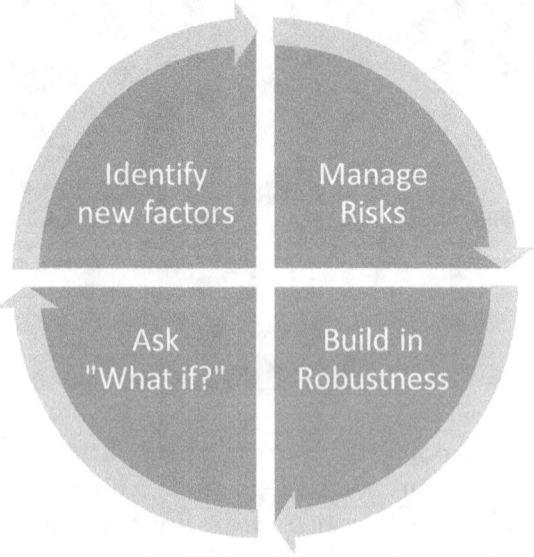

Figure 29 - The "what if?" cycle

Emergent Risk is inherently linked to change in circumstances and the appearance of new information. So the management of Emergent Risk must be linked to how change in the project is managed. Deterministic project management views change as a response to an Issue (an unplanned event). Traditionally change is also usually to be avoided or resisted. The Issue occurs, if necessary the project plan is updated to reflect the change, approval is gained for the new plan and we are back on track. Effective management of Emergent Risk needs a shift in this responsive behaviour. Change needs to be anticipated as early as possible. To be sure we cannot know about black swans until Europeans reach Australia, but as soon as the first reports come back we can be thinking about how they will impact the project. When an eruption occurs, we can instantly assess the new Risk environment not wait to see if change results at a later point. And better still, we can build robustness into our planning. We can ensure perhaps that our project is not dependent on a key individual who is now stranded in the U.S.

"What if ?"

In their book "Great by choice", Collins and Hansen study companies which are at least ten times as successful as the average in their industry. So what makes a company so successful? They conclude that the ability to anticipate change and manage Emergent Risk is central to the success of these "great" companies. The companies cannot know what changes will occur, but they expect that there will be change and are fast to respond. In particular they have a "What if" attitude which is central to successful management of Emergent Risk.

> *The 10x winners … always assumed that conditions can unexpectedly change.*
> *They were hypersensitive to changing conditions, continually asking 'What if?'*
>
> *"Great By Choice - Uncertainty, Chaos, and Luck"*
> *Collins + Hansen*

The conclusion that a "What if?" attitude is key is not unexpected. Many writers who are studying changeable and unpredictable environments identify this as a key skill area. Few are more unpredictable than military environments, and the conclusion of military writers is often similar to that above. If the environment is likely to change unpredictably, then constant questioning is the best approach. You do not win a battle by comparing your plan line by line with the enemy's. You win by responding better to the enemy plan than he or she does to yours.

> *A general-in-chief should ask himself*
> *several times a day*
> *'What if the enemy were to appear now in my front,*
> *or on my right, or my left?'.*
>
> **Napoleon Bonaparte**

Collins and Hansen coined a phrase for this approach – "Productive Paranoia". This sums up the approach brilliantly. You need to look for change, for problems and for what will break your plan, but you need to do so in a way that brings you effective benefit. It is too easy to slip into a negative response "something will go wrong with the plan". This can then drive a negative view of planning, concluding "why plan if the plan cannot be relied on?" Instead, we need a constructive approach "something will go wrong so let's have a plan to deal with it". If you know there will be change, but cannot predict the details, you need to ensure your plans are robust – reduce the overall Risk level, maintain cash buffers, build in review points, whatever is needed.

Productive Paranoia

- Ask "What if?"
- Identify Risk
- Manage Risk
- Anticipate Problems
- Build Robustness

Negativity

- Ask "Why Plan?"
- Expect failure
- Poor planning
- Demotivation

Figure 30 - "Productive Paranoia" is a positive force

Chapter 8 Exercise – Your Risks

 Can you think of a past project where an unexpected Risk occurred? Think through the underlying cause. Was this a failure to identify a Risk or a true Emergent Risk? It's easy in hindsight to say "we should have thought of this", but could you really have done so?

When did the clues become apparent and how early could you have seen the Risk if you had asked "What if?"

Chapter 9

How agility can help

What is agility?

Planning may need more than the ability to identify Risks. As we have seen, Emergent Risk cannot be predicted. And with a static plan it can be hard to respond to Risk or to exploit Opportunities. In an environment where change is likely we need a different mindset. Instead of a plan which is developed at the start of the project and replanned only when events make it necessary, we need to think about frequent replanning. We need a "What if?" attitude. And we need the flexibility to respond and exploit. In short, we need agility.

> *Agile: able to move quickly and easily*
>
> **Oxford English Dictionary**

In a planning context, "agility" is the ability to change the plan quickly and easily. This allows you to respond swiftly to changing circumstances, whether Emergent Risk or Opportunities. Even more than this, agile Planning assumes that change will happen and plans in a way that allows the change to be exploited to gain the most value from the project.

agility is not (quite) an Agile methodology

The term "Agile Development" has many interpretations. It covers a range of specific methodologies, of which Scrum is probably the most well-known. The introduction of agility into planning borrows heavily from some of these approaches. Agility does not, however, require a specific Agile approach, and this book does not choose one. I would suggest you explore one or more of these if you want to move beyond the basics of agile Planning.

The Agile movement summarises its key focus areas in the statements below. It notes that *"while there is value in the items on the right, we value the items on the left more"*. As you will see these statements cover many topics, even without the further detail included in specific methodologies.

> *Individuals and interactions over processes and tools*
> *Working software over comprehensive documentation*
> *Customer collaboration over contract negotiation*
> *Responding to change over following a plan*
>
> **Agile Manifesto**

This book focusses on the fourth of these points. This is the value of responding to change over following a plan. And it makes a distinction between **a planning approach which is able to respond to change** and a specific Agile methodology. To indicate this, this book uses a lower case "a" for "agility". This indicates "agile Planning", meaning a planning approach which is flexible. There are many aspects of team management which are central to Agile approaches and to successful projects, but which are far beyond the scope of this book. Whatever approach you use, you need to spend most of your time understanding your team. You need to focus on how to make your team most effective, whatever techniques that team may need (maybe as below).

> *The powers of a man's mind are directly proportioned to the quantity of coffee he drinks*
>
> **Sir James Mackintosh**

Do we need to be agile?

Why would we want to change the plan quickly? That depends on the type of project which we are running and the implications of change. There is a continuum of project types here with different needs.

Sequential Projects

At one extreme we have sequential projects. These are typically characterized by a large number of interdependencies and a ground-up design, starting from nothing. Risk in these projects often comes from how the pieces work together, how you will test the integrated system, and how you will architect and design the overall output to get the best performance from all of the pieces together. The whole is often more than the sum of the parts. Developing a Space Shuttle might be an example of this type of project. When dealing with a complicated project there is often merit in designing the overall system with great care. Change is typically limited due to its implications on the whole system. This leads to planning out all of the activities starting with design and testing documents.

In the ChipCo environment, design projects were typical "sequential" projects. Each design is new, and features are inter-related. A product with partial functionality will typically not be useful. The product is fixed once implemented as a silicon "chip", which means that you cannot add new features and you have to have been very thorough testing the whole product.

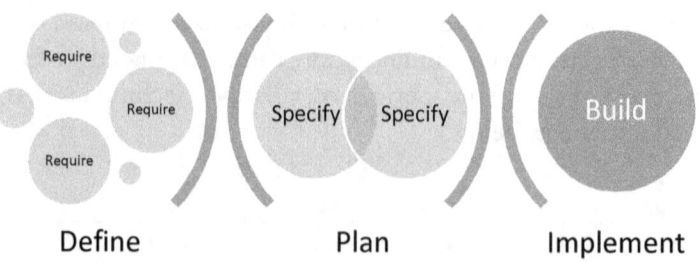

Define   Plan   Implement

Figure 31 - Sequential Project

Incremental Projects

At the other extreme we have incremental projects. These have an existing base development which is being extended by a number of small increments. An example might be a software product to which new features are added, but this could just as easily apply to a change programme. The increments are independent and can be done in any order. Typically benefits are delivered incrementally and the result is viable with any number of increments added. The independence of the features, the option to re-order them and the possibility of change all favour an agile approach.

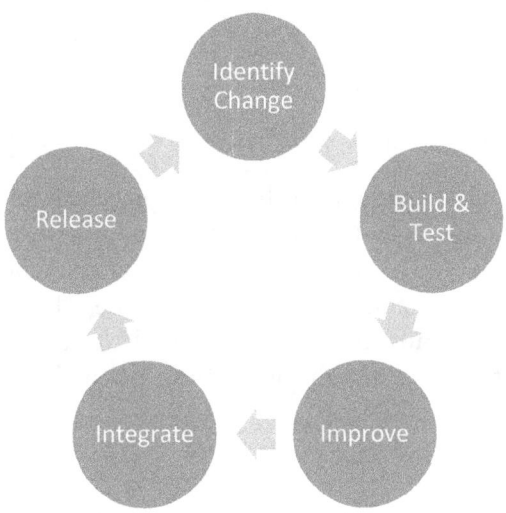

Figure 32 - Incremental Project

> *When I have worked with groups developing software tools, these are typical "incremental" products. If I buy a new word processor, I expect it to be maintained for years. There will be patches and bug fixes, maybe new functionality, support for new standards and interfaces. Perhaps less obviously, I have also tended to run change programmes in the same way. While keeping an overall vision and goal, benefits can be delivered incrementally. This allows early benefit realisation and reduces the impact of a big rollout.*

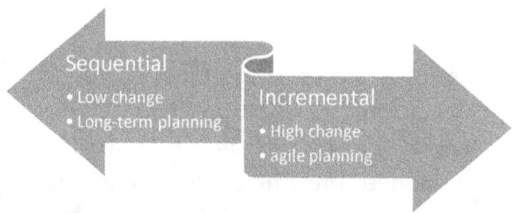

Figure 33- The spectrum of project types

> *A cat is very skilled at capturing its prey.*
> *But when its attention is focused, it can be easily*
> *caught with a net.*
> *On the other hand, a huge yak is not easily overcome.*
> *But for all its strength, it cannot catch a mouse.*
>
> ***Chuang Tzu***

There is no single "right approach" for all projects. As Chuang Tzu's quote suggests, the agile project is like a cat, able to reprioritize and chase down value with constant change but at risk when the changes have wide-reaching consequences through the whole development. The complicated and sequentially planned project is like the yak, unable to respond so nimbly but robust when the environment is stable.

Remember back to the "road crossing" example. We had an Issue when the footbridge was blocked and narrowly avoided one when the biscuits weren't available. Your child had to come back and ask what to do. This would be a formal change process in a project. But what if we had a better answer for some projects? With more flexibility and autonomy, perhaps we would have a robust project that could progress even with these problems.

Agile and Waterfall

The terms "Agile" and "Waterfall" are often used to describe the extremes of incremental and sequential projects. However, these have gained a large amount of "hidden" meaning from their usage over the years. There's also a substantial amount of perceived conflict with one or the other presented as "right". This is often due to badly-run implementations, or perhaps from people selling packaged solutions. "Agile" refers as much to self-managing teams as to planning approaches (as noted above in the four statements of the Agile Manifesto). "Waterfall" is an even less clearly defined concept. Possibly the first paper showing a "Waterfall" development flow (Royce, 1970) is not even to promote the approach but to argue for a level of iteration. To avoid the associated "baggage" it is useful to avoid emotive terms in favour of clearer descriptors such as "Sequential projects" or "Incremental projects".

What is an agile plan?

If we have "agile planning" then we must have an "agile plan". What does this look like? It is certainly not a full schedule of when all of the activities will be performed and by whom, running to the end of the project. But why not? Why does a complete schedule conflict with agility? If change is expected, then your confidence in a far-forward plan is low. And that means that the value of your far-ahead detailed planning is low. Looking at this as Value-driven Planning, there will be a horizon beyond which the cost of detailed planning is greater than the value of the plan. As we will see that doesn't mean there is no plan beyond this, but it is a less complete and detailed plan. Agility comes from including only the data which is valuable at any time and deferring other data until it is needed.

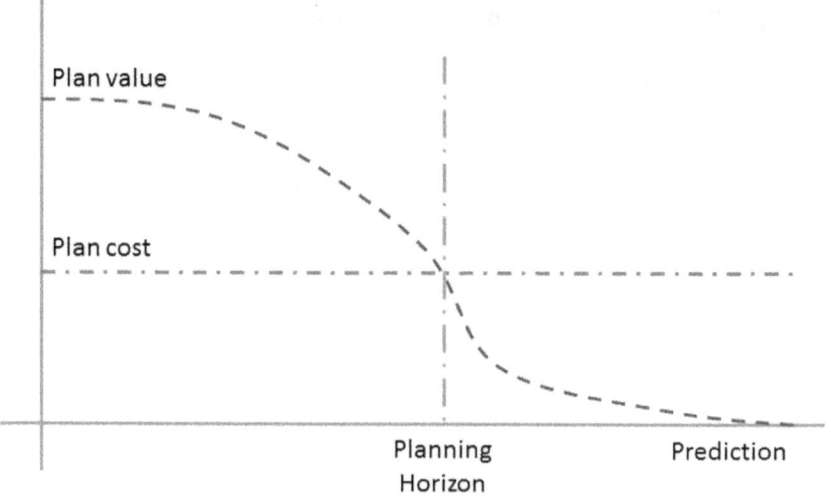

Figure 34 - Planning Horizon

> agile planning involves only creating as much planning data as has value at a point in time.

This necessarily means that the agile plan will evolve. New data is added as and when it is needed. The plan is no longer fixed and planning occurs throughout the project. The emphasis moves from the plan as a fixed artefact to the planning as an evolution. This gives the opportunity to realise benefits early and keep continual responsiveness to change by on-going planning as was suggested in the section on "Emergent Risk".

> *agile planning balances the effort and investment in planning with the knowledge that we will revise the plan through the course of the project.*
>
> **Mike Cohn, Agile Estimating and Planning**

An "agile plan" is **not** a complete schedule to the end of the project. So what is it? The plan has to satisfy two needs. Firstly the plan has to be sufficient to allow the team to make commitments and deliver value to the business. And secondly the plan has to be flexible enough to allow the business value to be maximised.

> An agile plan is a demonstration that all Commitments can be confidently achieved, and the business value maximised.

Unsurprisingly this sounds like a Risk management strategy. Certainly much more than it sounds like a fixed project schedule. It is not a demonstration of exactly *how* you will achieve the objectives over the whole project, it is an indication that you *can* do so at low Risk. To reduce the Risk you will need a detailed short term plan, but a less detailed longer term plan.

> *Prediction is very difficult, especially about the future*
>
> **Danish saying**

Components of an agile Plan

Agile planning uses a different set of naming and some different constructs. These can be confusing for those used to more traditional planning. So let us briefly explore three of the key components in building an agile plan – Backlog, Iteration and Commitment.

> *My experience has been that language can prove a barrier here. An agile plan uses terms which are not well understood by those working sequentially. This lack of shared understanding can make it difficult to communicate in environments with both sequential and incremental projects. However, using these terms has value because there is no alternative with exactly the same meaning. "Backlog" and "Iteration" are agile terms with no exact equivalent in sequential plans. "Commitment" is more a sequential planning term but one that is important to map to the agile plan.*

Backlog

A key feature of agile projects is that a partial delivery typically has value. A traditional plan has a fixed set of Requirements and declares success to be delivery of all of the mandatory Requirements. However an agile plan is expected to change. It has a set of Requirements **at a point in time**. We can deliver some of these and realise some value. But priorities may change, through imposed changes or a desire to exploit new Opportunities.

So the set of Requirements guides the current thinking but evolves over time. This set of Requirements is called "Backlog". Backlog is dynamic. There is no promise that all the current Backlog will be delivered, now or ever, but it represents the current best view of desired benefits.

> *Backlog: An accumulation of uncompleted work or matters needing to be dealt with*
>
> *Oxford English Dictionary*

Iteration

Agile planning implements detailed planning to a planning horizon. It then uses regular replanning as the horizon moves. This lets you implement planning and change with a simple replanning cycle. The cyclical nature of this approach has led to the name "iteration". Iterations are a subdivision of the project representing the part of the project which currently has a detailed plan of execution. You will often hear iterations referred to as "Sprints", although strictly this is the specific term for them in the Scrum methodology.

> *Iteration: The repetition of a process*
>
> **Oxford English Dictionary**

Iterations are generally of a fixed duration. The length of the iteration will depend on the anticipated level of change in the project. If the iterations are too long, the ability to respond to change will be lost. Either plans will be made and discarded, or change cannot be implemented until the iteration ends which may be some way in the future. Conversely if the iterations are too short, the rigour of planning will be lost. Typically iteration lengths for development projects will be around two to four weeks. However if the approach were used for a change programme, the iterations would probably be significantly longer.

Iterations should deliver value. They are more than milestones in a traditional project plan. The iteration should deliver some of the project value, through new features in a code base or measurable benefits in a change project.

Commitments

The business sets goals on a roadmap. Projects need to be able to make Commitments and deliver on them. Strategic planning depends on projects delivering on their promises to achieve the business needs. This is true whether the project is delivering features in a software tool roadmap or change in an organizational change programme. Committing can be a challenge for deterministic planning but can be even more daunting when you are using agile Planning. You are planning with iterations and have a horizon at the end of the iteration beyond which you do not have a detailed plan. Does that mean that you can make no Commitments beyond the end of the iteration? That is not generally an option. Even if developing iteratively you still need to have a roadmap and to be able to commit that features will be delivered at some point in the future. But how can you do this in the absence of a detailed project schedule?

Figure 35 – Planning cycles

Chapter 10

agile goal planning

Project goal, agile plan

Any project or programme starts with a vision. There is a desired goal for the project, whether this is a product being developed, or a change being implemented. A project cannot function wholly incrementally because it needs a direction and a strategy. The vision guides the Backlog, which is the benefits definition of what we currently want to achieve. The key benefits of the project are planned as a roadmap or top-level set of goals for the project. These are then implemented across multiple Iterations. This is the balance between planning and flexibility which allows an agile plan to deliver value and also to respond to change.

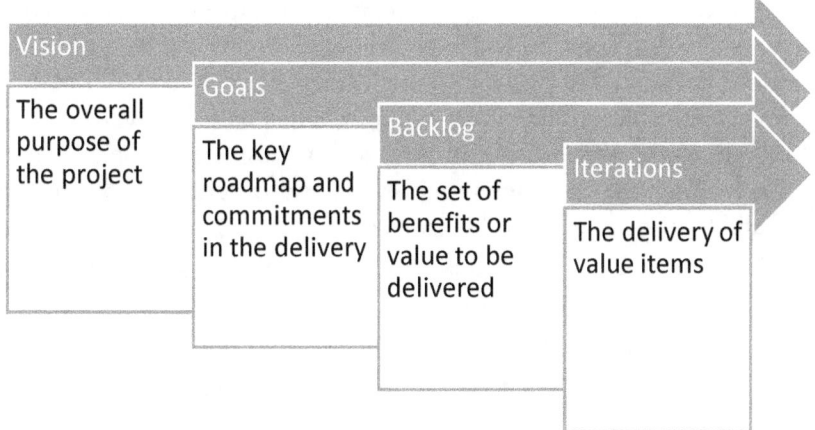

Figure 36 - Cascading the vision

Goals and commitments

It can be challenging for any team to make Commitments. This is even more the case when following an agile plan. The agile approach means that Backlog will be reordered with new items added and removed. The Backlog has no detailed task breakdown and levels of uncertainty will be high as a result. But the project still needs to commit to a roadmap of the key goals. The business will need to know when key benefits will become available and it needs to know more than one iteration ahead. This is true whether we are delivering a software product or a change programme.

There is a key secret of making successful Commitments from an agile plan. This is not to commit to everything currently on the Backlog. You are building a "backbone" to the plan, not a complete fixed schedule. Only a few key items on the Backlog will be committed to specific dates. You are looking to demonstrate that these are achievable. You know that will achieve more than these committed items. If you over-commit you lose flexibility and the whole point of the agile plan is lost.

Available effort

You need to understand how much effort you will have available for doing the work. This allows you to find the capacity of all of your iterations. Each iteration will have a defined duration and an assigned number of people so it has a certain capacity for work. But not everyone will be working fully on your Backlog. You will need to think about the overheads and how much these affect the available effort. All of the considerations below, and others, will reduce the availability of people from the project.

How much of each individual's time is assigned to your project and are they shared between projects?

What leave, training or absence will occur during the iteration?

How much effort will it take to manage the team?

What are the overheads for support, regressions, build system or other on-going activities?

Will people need time to spend on ramping up to speed?

This gives you an idea of how much effort is available in each of your iterations, perhaps as below, taking into account ramp-up and seasonality.

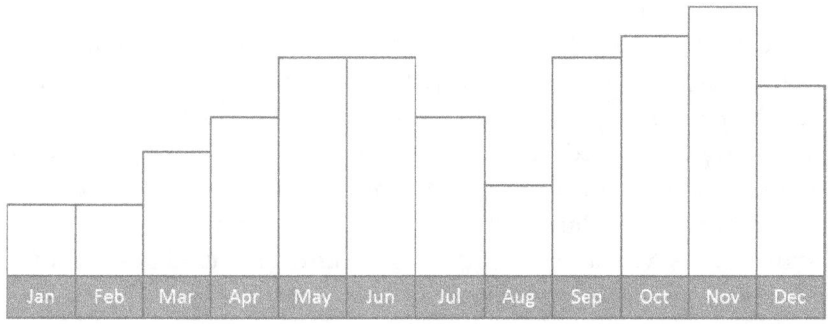

Figure 37 - Capacity by iteration

Required work

Now you need to size the Requirements on the Backlog which make up your Commitments. You want to obtain "most likely" and "worst case" estimates. Remember you don't have a detailed task breakdown, although you may need some level of breakdown and thought to come up with these numbers. So "worst case" estimates could be much larger than "most likely" at this stage. As long as you are looking at just the key Requirements this isn't a problem. Use the formula below to take the uncertainty into account.

("most likely") + ("worst case"-"most likely") / 4

I have found that one of the biggest challenges here can be the team's understandable reluctance to estimate. Their experience may be that the estimates are taken as hard fact, when the team know knowledge is limited. I like to talk about "sizing" at this stage, rather than "estimation". You can't accurately estimate without a task breakdown, and you aren't planning to that level in advance. But the team need to understand that their goals are achievable, and this is their chance to assess that.

Once you have estimates for those key Requirements that deliver the main project goals, think in which iterations they are likely to occur. There will probably be dependencies between Requirements and if these are kept in separate iterations that makes the plan robust. If you fit the estimates for those key Requirements into the available effort profile you will end up with something like the graph below. In this case there are key goals every three months shown with arrows. The Requirements to feed into those goals are spread across preceding iterations and shaded to match the arrows. The size of the Requirements is adjusted to take account of the "worst case" estimates. As we can see in this case, the effort required to deliver the key goals, even taking uncertainty into account, is below the capacity available, taking overheads into account. So we can be confident that these goals are achievable and can commit to them. We cannot be sure what other Requirements will be delivered from the extra capacity (in white) but we are committing only to the four specific goals that we have planned out.

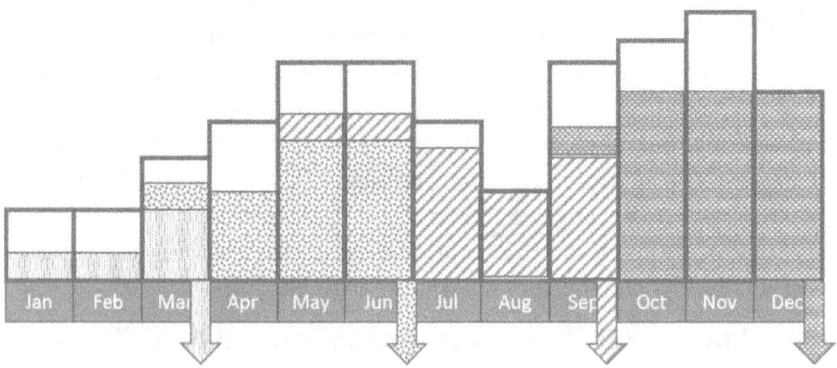

Figure 38 – Key Requirements by iteration

This now gives us a set of key goals for the project which we feel are realistic. There is no full schedule, but it is backed by:

A set of Requirements for each goal.

Sizing for these Requirements

Sequencing of dependent Requirements into iterations

An understanding of available capacity for iterations

This gives us a top-level achievable agile plan for what we can commit to delivering. Next we need to look at the detailed planning for how we will deliver this.

Chapter 11

agile iteration planning

Let us look at the planning of an iteration. This is the short-term planning process for what will be achieved in the next stage of the project. Planning an iteration is very similar to the planning of a complete deterministic project and uses many of the planning approaches that were discussed in the previous book. The sections below outline how these are applied in an agile plan.

Iteration definition

We start by agreeing the definition of the iteration. We need to understand the Requirements for the iteration, which come from the backlog. Remember that the backlog contains everything we would like to achieve in the project. Strictly this is everything we currently believe we would like to achieve, remember this will change over time. We won't manage all of this in the next iteration so we need a prioritization process. This will decide which are the most critical Requirements for this iteration. You can do this by ordering the Requirements, or by assigning them a score, or by giving them a priority using MoSCoW, rating Requirements into four categories.

- "Must Have" – these must be delivered from this iteration.
- "Should Have" – these are important and would be expected to be included, but could be delivered in a later iteration
- "Could Have" – these are useful and will be included in the planning but can be dropped in the execution if necessary.
- "Won't Have" – although these have value, it is agreed that these will not be included in this iteration.

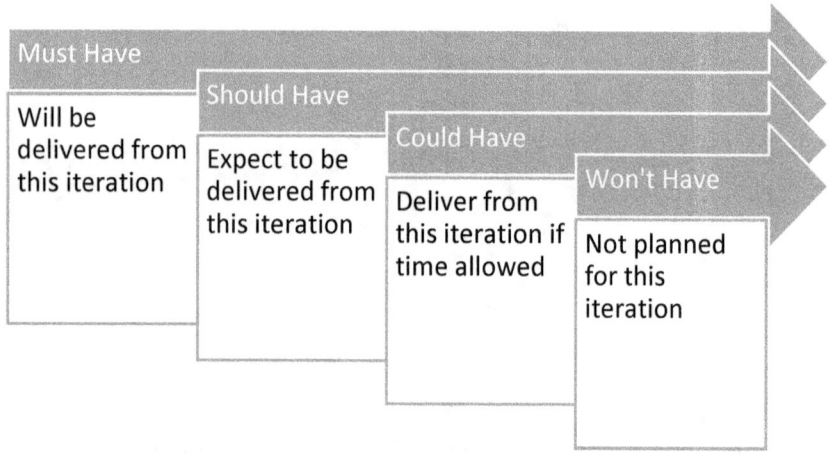

Figure 39 - MoSCoW prioritisation

Prioritisation is based on the value of the benefits which can be delivered immediately from this iteration. It is also based on the need to complete the Requirement in order to achieve a later goal. Remember that we have planned out the Requirements needed in each iteration as part of the goal planning. As with any project Requirements, this stage is likely to involve a complex stakeholder environment with conflicting prioritisations. It is critical to ensure that the objectives are agreed before the iteration begins. Success for this iteration will then be delivering the "Must Have" Requirements. As we will see we would also expect to deliver some or most of the "Should Have" Requirements, or our overall roadmap may fall behind. Since iterations are short you want to have a set of Requirements at the start which does not change. Iterations are quite robust and can tolerate some level of changing Requirements priorities, but this can lead to lack of clarity of success criteria.

An iteration should have a stable and agreed set of Requirements.

Whichever prioritization system you use, remember that the scoring is for the iteration planning. It is not a measure of how important the Requirement is for the project as a whole, but of how critical it is to complete the Requirement in the current iteration. For example, you could easily have a "Must Have" Requirement for the project as a whole that is not needed in this iteration.

Iteration planning

You need to make a plan for each Requirement being addressed in this iteration. That is no different from making a deterministic plan, although on a shorter timeframe. For each you need to consider the outputs needed, then the activities required to generate these and then estimate the size of each activity. There are a few ways however in which the planning process differs from deterministic planning.

Due to the short timescale and low level of dependencies, iterations do not generally schedule the tasks. It is generally sufficient to work from a task list. When a team member starts work on implementing a Requirement, they work through the set of tasks needed for that Requirement. So why is this approach adopted rather than a complete schedule? It is certainly one of the big contrasts between agile plans and more traditional planning, and an area of debate between those used to sequential planning and those favouring iterative planning.

Remember that agile planning is generally used for incremental projects. These typically have low levels of dependencies. The timeframe of an iteration is also short, so the amount of work involved is limited. The benefit from scheduling each task is therefore relatively low. The overhead can be high – given the short duration of an iteration, the amount of initial planning should be minimized.

Iteration estimation

As with any plan, the team need to be able to commit to achieving what is needed for the iteration. If there is a set of "Must Have" Requirements for the iteration, the team need to be confident that they can deliver these in that iteration. The process for achieving this confidence is identical to the approach for a deterministic plan.

The team must estimate the work involved at least in the "Must Have" Requirements. This typically involves breaking the Requirements down into a set of tasks needed to deliver the Requirements and estimating these tasks. As with deterministic planning, we expect to have "Most Likely" and "Worst Case" estimates for each Requirement. This implies a significant amount of planning work at the start of the iteration. It is tempting (as with all planning) to ignore estimation and instead to start on the implementation of Requirements. However, without the estimates we cannot be clear what is achievable in the iteration. This means that it will be difficult to demonstrate success

Available effort

We need to understand the effort which is available for Requirement implementation within the iteration. With a fixed iteration duration and typically a fixed team size over that short duration, that should be easy. But as with goal planning we need to think about the overheads of time which is not spent on addressing Requirements.

The table below is an example for a 2 week iteration with 10 people. In this example only 57 days of the 100 days effort potentially in the iteration are actually available for working on Requirements.

Activity	People needed	Days needed
Holiday		5
Working on other projects	0.5	5
Support	0.5	5
Build System	0.3	3
Iteration planning		5
Management	1.5	15
Release		5
TOTAL OVERHEAD		43
AVAILABLE DAYS		57

Buffering strategy

The big difference between agile planning and more traditional approaches is in how buffers are managed to ensure confident delivery. A traditional plan is schedule driven and implements buffering through schedule. This could be a very simple approach ("we may deliver late") or a more sophisticated approach with explicit buffers. These are schedule buffers which protect the project from overrun by committing to a date later than the plan date.

This approach is not effective for agile planning. The agile plan does not schedule the tasks. An iteration is generally fixed delivery. If the end date is set, a schedule buffer can't be used as there is no flexibility available. Instead, the buffering is imposed through flexibility on the features. That is why the feature prioritization is so important. Uncertainty in estimation will mean that you can't predict exactly **what** you have capacity to deliver, even though you know **when** it will be delivered. It is key to understand here that buffering is still present, even though the format is different.

Committing to the iteration

Now we have the estimates and the buffering strategy we can consider what we can commit to delivering in this iteration. One common mistake to avoid is to over-commit and fail. Alternatively teams may make no commitment at all, saying only that they will deliver "what they can" in the iteration. This doesn't lead to an agreed set of success criteria and so the team end up in the situation where it is unclear if they have been successful. Worst still, there is a lack of clarity about whether the top level vision is on track.

The estimates are used to build the plan for the iteration and to allow the team to answer the key planning questions for the iteration:

> Are we confident we can deliver all of the "Must Have" Requirements for this iteration?

> How many of the lower priority Requirements do we think we will also achieve?

Now we can put the pieces together to assess how much we can commit to achieving in the iteration. We will have more information than when we did the initial goal planning. However, we again need to build in the "Worst Case" estimates for, sizing each Requirement using the usual formula:

("most likely") + ("worst case"-"most likely") / 4

So we can work down the prioritized backlog adding up these adjusted estimates until the total reaches the effective available effort for the iteration. This is shown below. In this example, the "adjusted effort" taking into account the "Worst Case" estimates allows us to commit to all of the "Must Have" and two of the "Should Have" Requirements for this iteration. When the iteration is run, we will be likely to achieve more than this, but we are confident that these will be delivered in this iteration.

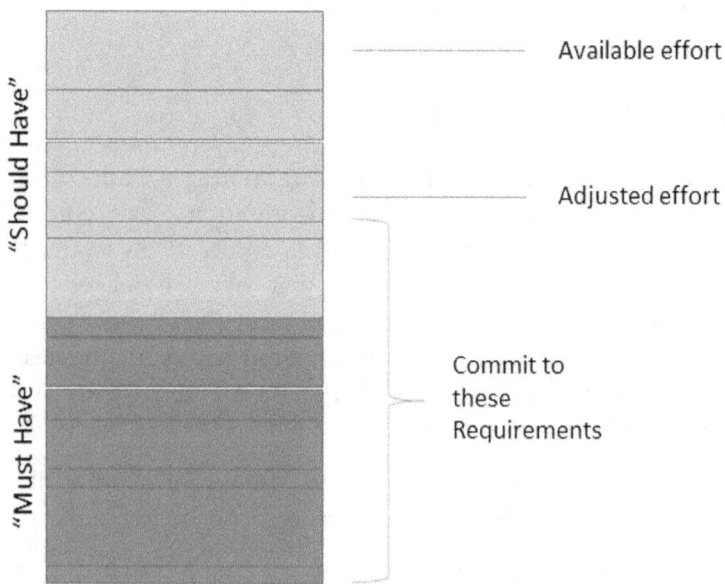

Figure 40 - Commitments for the iteration

An example is below. We have a two week iteration (ten days) and we have four people, we have 40 days of effort in the iteration. After taking account of the overheads, let's say we have 30 days. We have a Backlog as below at the start of the iteration, with estimates for each Requirement. The table shows "most likely" and "worst case" estimates, and also works out the weighted value using the formula above. We then show the total weighted work counting from the highest priority item. We can then commit to up to 30 days effort, which means we expect to complete the shaded Requirements up to number 7. This includes all of the "Must Have" Requirements which makes the iteration plan viable.

Req	Priority	Most Likely	Worst Case	Weighted	Total
1	Must Have	2	3	2.25	2.25
2	Must Have	3	5	3.5	5.75
3	Must Have	5	10	6.25	12.0
4	Must Have	2	3	2.25	14.25
5	Must Have	5	10	6.25	20.5
6	Should Have	3	5	3.5	24.0
7	Should Have	3	5	3.5	27.5
8	Should Have	5	10	6.25	33.75
9	Should Have	1	1	1	34.75
10	Should Have	5	10	6.25	41.0

Retrospective

An iteration should deliver value. At the end of the iteration we need to review the progress. We committed to deliver some Requirements. Did we do so? What have we learned? What went well and what went badly? How does this change the progress on overall project goals?

The reason for adopting an iterative approach is because we expect high levels of change. This review point, often called a "Retrospective" is therefore not an optional item but a key part of managing the change. This is the "What if?" point at which you look at what has changed and how it impacts the project as a whole. How have your achievements moved you on towards your goal? Are you still on track? What new Risks are there? Perhaps what you have learned means that the goals themselves are changing.

One key purpose of a retrospective is also to judge when we can end the project. If we have achieved the initial project goals, we may wish to continue with the current Backlog. But if we have achieved enough benefit that the next iteration will not add significant further value, it is time to end.

Velocity

In an agile plan we can use the Retrospective to assess speed of progress. At the start of the iteration we have estimated the Requirements and the available effort. At the end of the iteration we review progress against our estimates. We can start to produce a figure which maps estimates to delivery, and this is called "velocity", indicating how fast we can deliver Requirements.

Our Retrospective may be able to give us some of the causes. But the purpose is not judgemental. Perhaps we can understand that we are spending more effort on Support, or that we are underestimating some areas. But the purpose is to improve, not to criticise.

Let us look back at the table of Requirements above. We initially estimated that with ten days and four people, we could deliver up to Requirement 7. Perhaps we only delivered the "Must Have" items, up to Requirement 5. So we delivered 20.5 days of estimated effort in the iteration. Perhaps we underestimated some tasks. Perhaps the overheads were more than we expected.

Whatever the reason, we can say that our Velocity is here 20.5/40 or 0.51 estimated days of work completed per available day of effort. We can use this as a starting point to assess what we should commit to in future. Next iteration, assuming it is again 40 days of effort, we can again expect to deliver 20.5 estimated days of work.

What is elegant about this approach is that it is self-correcting. Velocity takes account of overheads and estimation bias in a feedback loop that measures what is actually delivered. You start with an initial expectation for overheads and speed of delivery, but you can adjust this as you progress. In a deterministic plan you don't have the option to reprioritize based on real measures in this way. However, it is important that you measure consistently. If there is a change in resourcing, for example, your velocity for the next iteration will be different. And as a team improves their estimation, the velocity will again change.

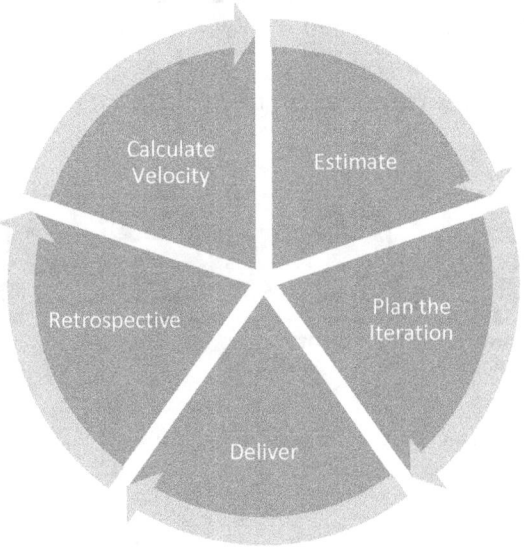

Figure 41 - The agile estimation cycle.

Chapter 12

Conclusion

Why Risk Management works.

The previous book looked at planning in stable environments. As environments become more changeable, new techniques are needed. This book has looked at how to work with those changeable projects. You still need a good plan, but there are new approaches to master as well. You need to be able to anticipate what may go wrong and manage Risk to ensure you can prevent problems. You need to build flexibility into your plan to be able to respond to changing needs and to exploit opportunities. And you need to cultivate a "What if ?" approach to see your plan as an ever-changing guide, not a fixed predictor. There is a fine line to draw in using Risk Management positively. This is not about saying every project will fail, but about seeing the problems early enough to fix them.

Determinism   Uncertainty   Agility   Risk

Figure 42 – Four Horsemen slain

Epilogue

 *At ChipCo there were many skilled project teams who could create amazing products. Fewer teams had the experience to produce good plans. These teams could identify everything they needed to do and build a credible approach to achieve it.*

But a very few teams were able to spot the problems coming. They followed the "What if ?" approach, built flexibility into the plan, they thought about what might go wrong and they had an answer before there was a problem.

It's easy to see Risk Management as just going through the motions. I remember one training delegate saying after a course "I've been asked for years to identify Risks, but this is the first time anyone has discussed what that means". This book is due to him and to all the others that I have worked with to understand what it does mean.

The quote below from Antoine de Saint-Exupery, writer and adventurer, shows how to deal with changeable environments. And the difference between good management and great management is all about Value.

> *If you want to build a ship, don't drum up the men to gather wood, divide the work and give orders.*
> *Instead, teach them to yearn for the vast and endless sea.*
> *As for the future, your task is not to foresee it, but to enable it*
>
> ***Antoine de Saint-Exupery***

Value-driven Principles of Risk

I have highlighted the following which constitute key principles of Value-driven Risk Management. These are key places to focus your limited time and effort because they will make a difference. As in the last book, in deference to Deming's 14 rules for Total Quality Management, I have kept to 13 for Value-driven Risk and agility.

1. Project Management skills are valuable and applicable to everyone working on projects.

2. Risk is invisible.

3. Risk Management is about maintaining a reasonable degree of confidence that project objectives will be achieved successfully.

4. There should be no occasion when a problem is known with no decision taken of how it should be acted on.

5. A Risk can be described as an event with an uncertain outcome and a resulting effect on the project.

6. Risk Identification should ensure that everyone's concerns are heard.

7. Risk Assessment allows you to build a prioritisation strategy.

8. It is better to manage key Risks well than to overload yourself with every conceivable Risk.

9. Reports should be focussed on Residual Risk.

10. Stakeholders need to be comfortable with the level of Risk.

11. agile planning involves only creating as much planning data as has value at a point in time.

12. An agile plan is a demonstration that all Commitments can be confidently achieved, and the business value maximised.

13. An iteration should have a stable and agreed set of Requirements.

Chapter 13

Answers to Exercises

Chapter 4 Exercise – Example Risks

You were asked to look at three potential Risks and plot them on a Risk Exposure Grid.

Possible Patent Issue.

The impact of this Risk is Critical as it prevents the project achieving its goals. The probability is Low as it has not been seen actually to occur on other projects.

New customer brings extra work

The impact of this Risk is Low as it can be accommodated by replanning. The probability is High as it seems to occur on half of similar projects.

Lead Engineer has left

This one is something of a trick. This is an event which has occurred and is therefore not a Risk at all but an Issue.

		Impact			
		Critical	High	Medium	Low
Likelihood	Very High				
	High				New Customer
	Medium				
	Low	Patent Issue			

Chapter 4 Exercise – Risk Distribution

In this exercise you were working with a group which had Risks distributed as below after Risk Analysis. Of course this may genuinely reflect the mix of Risks which have been found, but are there any concerns about this distribution which could be discussed further with the team?

		Impact			
		Critical	High	Medium	Low
Likelihood	**Very High**	0	1	10	20
	High	0	3	10	30
	Medium	1	10	40	10
	Low	2	4	10	30

Some areas which might lead to further discussion are marked on the diagram.

1. 22% of Risks are raised as Medium Likelihood, Medium Impact. It is possible that "Medium" has been used so often because the categories are not well understood.
2. 50% of Risks in the four bottom right cells (Low/Medium Likelihood, Low/Medium Impact). This could lead to a large management overhead for little value.
3. 50% of Risks are Low Impact. These may be low value and may indicate a focus on task uncertainty rather than on true Risk.
4. 17% of Risks are Very High Likelihood. These are areas where the plan will probably be affected by the Risk. This suggests perhaps the Risk management is not being effective.
5. Only 1% of Risks are Critical. Possibly the team are not identifying the real problems which could cause the project to fail.

Chapter 5 Exercise – Exploiting Opportunity

You were asked to look at an example Opportunity and how you might exploit this. We know that a major competitor is considering leaving the market and we raise an Opportunity as below:

There is an Opportunity that	*Our main competitor abandoning this market*	*will occur*	*and will result in*	*Increased customers and sales.*

To exploit this Opportunity we need a plan to increase its Likelihood or Impact. We may be able to discuss directly with the competitor in a way that increases the Likelihood, but the most likely plans will affect Impact. If the competitor leaves the market there will be an increased number of ***potential*** customers. The plan would need to assess how we would convert these to sales, with a marketing plan and ensuring sufficient resourcing on sales and support to deal with the possible increase.

	Risk Name	Vulnerability Category
Risk Identification	There is a risk that…	Causing…
	Risk Description	

	Likelihood	☐ Low ☐ Medium ☐ High ☐ Very High
Risk	Impact	☐ Low ☐ Medium ☐ High ☐ Critical

Risk Management	Preventative Actions
	Limiting Actions
	Residual Risk
	Likelihood ☐ Low ☐ Medium ☐ High ☐ Very High
	Impact ☐ Low ☐ Medium ☐ High ☐ Critical

Risk	Stakeholders – who is interested in this Risk?
	Response level ☐ Project ☐ Program ☐ Strategic